John McKenna, the editor of this memoir, is the grandson of Head Constable John McKenna. A Civil Servant based in Belfast, he has a long-term interest in genealogy and family history. Other interests include creative writing. As a second son and in the Irish tradition, he was named after his father's father. Although born long after his grandfather had died, his interest in his RIC ancestor down the years has culminated in having *A Beleaguered Station* published. His current wider interest in the period of Irish history covered by the memoir resulted from research conducted in order to better understand his grandfather's experiences.

A Beleaguered Station

The Memoir of Head Constable
John McKenna
1891–1921

A Catholic RIC Officer's
Experience of Violence
and Partition in Ulster

JOHN McKENNA

ULSTER HISTORICAL FOUNDATION

Community Relations Council

This book has received financial support from the Northern Ireland Community Relations Council which aims to promote a pluralist society and encourage an acceptance and an understanding of cultural diversity. The views expressed do not necessarily reflect those of the Council.

Ulster Historical Foundation is pleased to acknowledge support for this publication from the Belfast Natural History and Philosophical Society.

First published 2009, reprinted 2021
by Ulster Historical Foundation
www.ancestryireland.com
www.booksireland.org.uk

Except as otherwise permitted under the Copyright, Designs and Patents Act 1988, this publication may only be reproduced, stored or transmitted in any form or by any means with the prior permission in writing of the publisher or, in the case of reprographic reproduction, in accordance with the terms of a licence issued by The Copyright Licensing Agency. Enquiries concerning reproduction outside those terms
should be sent to the publisher.

© John McKenna

ISBN: 978-1-913993-07-8

Printed by Lightning Source
Design and typesetting by FPM Publishing

CONTENTS

ACKNOWLEDGEMENTS	vii
FOREWORD	ix
ABBREVIATIONS	xi
INTRODUCTION BY ÉAMON PHOENIX	xii
FAMILY BACKGROUND	xx
Author's Original Preface – The Eucharistic Congress 1932	1
Halcyon Days in the West: Galway to Carnlough	17
First signs of trouble: Larne to Kerry	26
Cookstown: into a flaming cauldron	37
Rock and a hard place the Joseph Hayden killing	55
'Running Amok': McAdoo's Car	73
Conclusion	90
A SEQUENCE OF HISTORICAL EVENTS	97
BIBLIOGRAPHY	102
INDEX	104

Acknowledgements

My biographical sketch of John McKenna and footnotes relating to this memoir could not have been completed without the help of various family members: my cousin Mary who provided information and advice relating to the family background, along with some of the photos used as illustrations; my sister and brother-in-law Teresa and William who provided the Linen Hall Library subscription; my brother Paddy for the invaluable technical support; my second cousin James Ward for photographs and background information; not forgetting the other family members who offered encouragement and assistance.

Particular thanks are due to the previous generation: my godmother Aunt Pauline, John's 99 year old daughter, who made available my grandfather's original memoir. Sadly, Pauline did not live to see this memoir published, as she died on 16 February 2009 (R.I.P.). Also John's niece Pat White, who died in September 2009 in her late nineties. She and her family made available relevant letters from the late-nineteenth and early-twentieth century.

I also acknowledge those long departed, not least Aunt Comgall. A member of the Congregation of the Sisters of St. Louis, she tried unsuccessfully in her lifetime to have her father's recollections published. Last but by no means least, I acknowledge my grandfather John McKenna himself, without whose gripping but all too short narrative of events long gone this book would certainly not have been published.

In the more recent past, I acknowledge the encouragement provided by Joe Woods in the 1980's, and the support given by my cousin Margaret in the early years of the present decade.

In the present day, special thanks must go to Dr Éamon Phoenix, without whose support and encouragement this publication would not have happened. His enthusiasm and vast knowledge of Irish history of the period covered in the book inspired me to persevere with the project. Also thanks to Fintan Mullan and the staff of the Ulster Historical Foundation for their support in the critical period leading up to publication.

JOHN McKENNA
Grandson of the author

Foreword

AS A GRANDSON OF JOHN MCKENNA also called John McKenna, I first came across this memoir around 20 years ago. It had been passed down almost by accident, his longhand narrative in the front of a notebook which had since been used by one of his daughters to collect unrelated memorabilia. This daughter was Kathleen, also known as Sister Mary Comgall, a member of the Congregation of the Sisters of St. Louis. She tried unsuccessfully to have the memoir published in the 1960's, but no one at that time was interested.

The entire memoir survived intact, although a few words towards the end were made illegible through wear and tear. There was much more John could have said to explain the situation he found himself in during his time in Cookstown, but for reasons we will never now know he chose not to.

Publication of the memoir was a vague ambition back in the mid-1980's, put on the back burner until now. Part of the reason for this was an awareness of the political sensitivities which might be ruffled even after so many years. Even more years have passed now, and the apparent dawning of a new era of peace and reconciliation in Northern Ireland encouraged me to think that some aspects of our history would now be viewed with greater objectivity.

The memoir as written by John follows a loose chronological narrative, although at times he does flit backwards and forwards. An exception to the chronological narrative is John's use of events relating to the Eucharistic Congress in Larne in 1932 as his starting point in the memoir. Although this may be initially confusing to the reader, it is important to remember that it was the sectarian attacks on the Larne procession which triggered John's recollections about his career in the RIC. Without the Congress, there would have been no memoir, and readers of Irish history today would be all the poorer for that. I have retained his continuity and the details are exactly as he wrote them, apart from punctuation, paragraphs and the like. Where occasionally his writing is illegible I have highlighted this, and where he has deliberately left out the names of places or individuals I have followed suit. I have attempted to put the memoir in context, using additional material from my own reading of Irish history for the period covered.

This book is dedicated to the memory of John McKenna in the belief that his life was not lived in vain. He coped as best he could with the difficulties he encountered, particularly towards the end of his RIC career. His family was his first priority, and he mentions in the memoir the sacrifice he made on their behalf by continuing as an RIC man in difficult circumstances. In acknowledgement of this, the book is also dedicated to John and his wife Katie's descendants and their families.

Abbreviations

DI – The District Inspector was in charge of the police district, which was usually a sub-division of the County. He would have been McKenna's immediate superior when he was promoted Head Constable.

CI – The County Inspector was in overall command of the police County district, and was the District Inspector's immediate superior.

'A' Specials – established as part of the Ulster Special Constabulary by the British government in October 1920, they were full-time police reservists used by the fledgling Northern Ireland administration to counter Republican activities as partition came about.

'B' Specials – paid part-time reservists who could be called upon by the RIC as required; established as part of the Ulster Special Constabulary in October 1920. They often operated without the sanction of the RIC command. There was also an unpaid reserve of 'C' Specials, civilians who could be called upon in an emergency.

Introduction

THIS MANUSCRIPT CONSISTS OF THE MEMOIR (around 16,000 words) of John McKenna (1870–1943) dealing with his career as a Catholic RIC officer *c.* 1891–1921 with particular emphasis on his almost 20 years in the north of Ireland spanning the Irish Revolution, partition and the 'Troubles' of 1920–21.

The memoir originated in ex-Head Constable McKenna's personal experience of the attack on pilgrims (including himself) as they prepared to leave Larne, Co. Antrim by boat for the Eucharistic Congress in Dublin in 1932 and the failure of the RUC to protect them. The manuscript opens with a graphic account of his experiences of the Larne attack and the subsequent public controversy, and moves on to reflect on the author's 30-year career in the old Royal Irish Constabulary in different parts of Ireland, culminating in a series of postings in Antrim and Tyrone during 1903–21.

The RIC had its origins in the Irish Constabulary, a military-style force, formed by Thomas Drummond, the Irish Under Secretary, in 1836. The force was granted the prefix 'Royal' for its role in suppressing the Fenian Rising of 1867. Members of the RIC were recruited from the tenant-farmer class. As a result, Catholics comprised some 80 per cent of the rank and file until its disbandment in 1922 with Protestants dominating the higher echelons. From its inception the higher ranks were directly commissioned from former military officers. This practice was relaxed from 1895 when the government decided that half of the district inspectors should be promoted from the ranks.

The RIC was headed by an Inspector General and was under the direct control of the Chief Secretary's Office in Dublin Castle. The British government saw the police force as:

a highly disciplined and well-educated body of men, spread over the whole face of the country in a web of which every thread centres on Dublin.[1]

Officers were not permitted to serve in their native counties and were transferred on promotion.

The primary function of the RIC was the maintenance of law and order in the country. While keeping the peace in a largely agricultural society was normally uneventful, it could involve crushing armed insurrection (on three occasions – 1848, 1867 and 1916) or dealing with serious agrarian agitation during the Land War of 1879–81. In the industrial north east, particularly Belfast, sectarian rioting required the attentions of the RIC in 1872, 1886 and the prolonged disturbances of 1920–22 which accompanied partition and the IRA campaign against British rule.

In Nationalist Ireland the police were caricatured in republican propaganda as the dark, brutal upholders of tyranny despite their roots in the native population. This did not make them any more popular with the loyalists of the industrial north. In the 1886 anti-Home Rule riots in Belfast the mainly Catholic police were dubbed 'Morley's Murderers' by the loyalists of the Shankill Road.[2]

Thus, while the RIC undertook ordinary everyday duties such as investigating petty crime, collecting agricultural statistics and pursuing poteen makers, they also served as the 'eyes and ears' of Dublin Castle on the ground. The regular monthly reports from the County Inspectors gave the Chief Secretary a unique insight into changes in political opinion, subversive influences, incidents of boycotting, trade union activities and the range of secret societies from the Orange Order and the Ancient Order of Hibernians to the IRB, and the rise of the Ulster Volunteer Force (UVF) and the Irish Volunteers after 1913. The reports also charted the sentiments of the local population on such key issues as Home Rule, the prospect of 'exclusion'/partition, the Easter Rising and the Conscription Crisis of 1918.

John McKenna was a typical recruit to the RIC at the end of the nineteenth century. Born in Co. Monaghan into a small farming family in 1870, he saw 'nothing dishonourable in joining the police'. He recalls that, like many of his fellow Catholic officers, he had little sense of Irish history though he adhered to the moderate Home Rule politics of John Redmond. He recalls an idyllic 12 years in the west of Ireland (where he married) before his transfer to Ballymena in the heart of Unionist Ulster in 1903. In the north, he found his religion a barrier to promotion though he was able to rise eventually to the rank of Head Constable through competitive examination.

In Carnlough, in the Glens of Antrim during the 'Ulster Crisis' of 1914 McKenna found himself under pressure from Unionist-minded superiors to find evidence of UVF drilling which was non-existent in the integrated village. The aim of the Unionist ruling class within the RIC was, he asserts, 'to frighten Asquith [the British Liberal prime minister] with the size of the [Ulster] Volunteers' army' and thus frustrate the hopes of nationalists like himself of Irish self-government under the third Home Rule Act which became law in September 1914.

Transferred to the port of Larne in 1914, he abhorred the failure of the police to seize the illegal UVF arms during the dramatic gun-running of that April and contrasted their inertia with the use of force by British troops against the Irish Volunteers during the much smaller arms importation at Howth two months later. The failure of the police to act against the UVF signalled the Catholic officer's dwindling faith in the impartiality of the RIC.

Significantly, McKenna is silent on the dramatic events of Easter 1916, the execution of the insurgent leaders and the subsequent wave of sympathy which swept across Nationalist Ireland. In the northern nationalist community, the RIC reported how, after the executions of Pearse and his comrades, 'the original feeling of distrust and annoyance changed as time went on and a feeling of sympathy with the rebels arose.'[3] In Unionist circles, however, the insurrection was viewed as a 'stab in the back' of Britain and the empire in time of war and a sample of what might be expected to transpire if Home Rule were implemented.

For his part, McKenna had no sympathy with the Rising but clearly shared the prevailing nationalist view that the Unionist leadership had created the conditions for rebellion and that 'Carson rekindled the Fenian flame.'[4]

The Sinn Féin landslide in the December 1918 general election saw the establishment of the First Dáil in January 1919 as the proclaimed parliament of an Irish Republic. On the day the Dáil met, 21 January 1919, a party of Irish Volunteers shot dead two RIC men at Soloheadbeg, Co. Tipperary. These shots marked the opening of the Anglo-Irish War (1919–21) in which the Volunteers, renamed the IRA, waged a relentless guerrilla warfare against the police and military. Over the next two years of conflict the police bore the brunt of both IRA attacks on isolated barracks and ostracisation by the civilian population. The result was a collapse in morale, mass resignations and the reinforcement of the force in 1920 by the Black and Tans, ill-disciplined ex-soldiers, and the Auxiliaries, an elite formation of former officers.

In October 1920 the British government acceded to Sir James Craig's demand for the enlistment of the pre-war UVF in an auxiliary police force, the Ulster Special Constabulary (USC).[5] By March 1922 this sectarian militia numbered 32,000 men in its full-time, part-time and reserve sections and was armed and financed by Westminster. The deployment of the new force caused tensions in the highly-disciplined RIC. But it was regarded with fear and disdain by the northern nationalist population. In the words of a senior Whitehall official, S.G. Tallents, sent to report on the situation in the north in 1922,

> the Catholics regard them with a bitterness exceeding that which the Black and Tans inspired in the south and several Unionist public men told me that this purely partisan and insufficiently disciplined force was sowing feuds ... which would not be eradicated for generations.[6]

The adoption of a 'reprisals' policy by the Lloyd George coalition in Ireland merely alienated the civilian population from British rule and placed honourable officers like John McKenna in a most invidious position. As Patrick Shea, a Stormont civil servant whose father served in the RIC during this violent period commented:

The men of the Royal Irish Constabulary had not the background or the disposition which produces heroes; they were quite unfitted for the part which they were called upon to fill by those who saw a resort to violence as the way to the attainment of the Ireland they wanted.[7]

During the conflict of 1919–21, McKenna saw service in the proclaimed counties of the south and spent a brief period in 1920 as Head Constable in Kenmare, Co. Kerry, 'the most dangerous county in Ireland'. He describes how he was unmolested despite attending daily Mass unarmed and in police uniform at the height of the guerrilla war.

The most detailed part of the memoir deals with the Head Constable's 'sickening' experiences in Cookstown, Co. Tyrone during 1920–22, which witnessed the establishment of the Northern Ireland state (June 1921), the Treaty of December 1921 and the spiral of political and sectarian violence in the north. McKenna was appalled by the deeply sectarian attitudes of some of his superiors, including the District Inspector, and, in particular, by what he saw as the official cover-up of sectarian murders carried out by the newly formed B Specials. He writes: 'As to the Black and Tans, I found them perfect gentleman in comparison to the Ulster Specials'. The 'Tans' were much more easily controlled by the police than the Specials, mainly local loyalist farm hands and labourers, he notes.

In a graphic account, McKenna describes how his District Inspector and the Cookstown Specials plotted against him, how raids on the homes of inoffensive Catholics were *de rigueur* 'to keep the B men quiet', and how his own life was constantly in danger from the USC. He relates in detail the brutal murder by Specials of a young Catholic farmer, Joseph Hayden, in his home near Cookstown in May 1921 and of high-level involvement in the shielding of the murderers. In relation to these events, McKenna wrote after a lapse of 11 years:

> I saw how helpless I was in being compelled to assist in committing such outrages on decent, inoffensive people. It was horrible to think that, after having spent 30 years in

what I thought to be an honourable job, to find it so rotten and having ... to take part in such foul deeds.

McKenna's concerns at the apparent ability of the Specials in east Tyrone to carry out sectarian attacks, including murder, with impunity, are corroborated by other reliable sources. In November 1921, Dr James Gillespie, a medical doctor and Coroner in Cookstown informed de Valera, president of the Dáil, of the 'depredations' of the Specials in the district. Their actions had convinced him that the new Unionist government of James Craig was 'trying to put down with the mailed fist all who oppose them.' Following the Treaty in February 1922 Gillespie wrote to Michael Collins, now chairman of the pro-treaty Provisional Government, protesting at fresh murders committed by the Specials in Tyrone.

Perhaps the most damning indictment of the USC in the county in McKenna's time here comes from two senior police sources. General A. Ricardo, who had organised the UVF in Co. Tyrone in 1920, told Tallents that he had joined the B force on its inception but resigned 'owing to their partisanship'. The force was drawn exclusively from the Protestant population 'and mainly from the more extreme side'. He reported that the lack of control resulted in 'much offensive repression' while 'criminal acts by the B Specials ... are "cloaked" and evidence is unobtainable'.[8]

Ricardo's colleague, Major Robert Stevenson, had resigned his post as district commandant of the B Specials in Dungannon in June 1922 because of indiscipline and sectarian bias in the force. He told Tallents:

> There can never be any ... confidence or stability as long as the B force, the ordinary Protestant countryman and in many cases "cornerboy" is supplied with arms ... and authorised to get on top of his Roman Catholic neighbour. The latter resents it all the time and even the most respectable and constitutional nationalist gets more bitter as the record of raids and abuses by the uncontrollable elements piles up and harmless and innocent people suffer ...[9]

This is a remarkable account which gives us a real insight into the life and experience of a moderate, loyal Catholic RIC officer from a Home Rule background in the RIC during the violence and upheaval of the Irish Revolution and partition. McKenna constantly stresses his total opposition to physical force and condemns the use of violence by both the UVF and IRA. His sympathies lie with the ordinary constable on the beat who became a legitimate target after 1919. His abiding regret was that, despite his faithful service in the force, he was undermined and distrusted by sectarian elements in the police in the north. Writing in 1932, he regretted the violence which had resulted in a partitioned Ireland and second class citizenship for northern Catholics.

This is the first autobiographical account by a Catholic nationalist RIC officer of the 1914–21 period. The only other first hand memoir is that of County Inspector John Regan, a Catholic Unionist, while Patrick Shea nostalgically recalls growing up as the son of a Catholic RIC man in a series of postings during the same tumultous period in Irish history.

What gives this memoir additional importance is the fact that it was inspired by the sectarian events of 1932 in Larne and elsewhere in Northern Ireland which McKenna, an organiser of the Catholic pilgrimage, experienced at first hand.

The result is a timely and useful book. It sheds new light on the deep-rooted nature of sectarianism in Northern Irish society, the dilemma of moderate nationalists like McKenna in the RIC in the early 1920s and the historic difficulty (now being resolved) of ensuring nationalist support for policing in a divided society.

ÉAMON PHOENIX
Principal Lecturer in History
Stranmillis University College

Notes

1. R.B. McDowell, *The Irish Administration 1801–1914* (London, 1964), pp. 143–4.

2. Ibid., pp. 143–4.

3. RIC Report for Belfast, 1916, National Archives (Kew), CO 904/120/3.

4. Michael Laffan, *The Partition of Ireland, 1911–1925* (Dundalk, 1983), p. 32.

5. M. Farrell, *Arming the Protestants: The Formation of the Ulster Special Constabulary and the Royal Ulster Constabulary 1920–27* (London, 1983), p. 153.

6. K. Middlemas (ed), *Thomas Jones, Whitehall Diary III: Ireland 1918–25* (Oxford, 1971), p. 38.

7. P. Shea, *Voices and the Sound of Drums: An Irish Autobiography* (Belfast, 1981), p. 81.

8. Farrell, op. cit., pp. 156–7.

9. Ibid.

Family Background

This memoir concerns John McKenna, born the second son of a farmer in Co. Monaghan in 1870. He joined the Royal Irish Constabulary as a Constable, aged 20 years and 3 months when appointed on 02 March 1891. For John, like many others before and since, the police represented an escape from the drudgery of farm labouring or the perils of emigration. Although the RIC enforced British writ in Ireland, and received the Royal title in 1867 as thanks for helping in the suppression of the Fenians, many ordinary Irishmen like John found that joining up did not conflict with their loyalty to either family or country.

Other Irishmen thought differently, as illustrated by a speech in the British House of Commons by the Irish Home Rule MP, Alfred Webb, who spoke in 1890 of the 'irresponsible Bashi-Bazouk action of the police in Ireland', describing the RIC as 'an incubus upon all civil life with no effective control over it. It is a Force which, though nominally Irish, is not Irish in feeling or tradition or any of its connections. It is among us, but not of us.' (*Hansard* 3, cccxlvi, 1149–50, 08 July 1890.)

John's early years in Galway before going to Ulster seem to have been relatively idyllic, but even then the northern part of the country cast its shadow over simple pleasures, as evidenced by a letter of the time written by his father-in-law:

> ... about Katie, now Mrs McKenna of Ardrahan, near Gort, Co. Galway. Mazie * had a letter and a new gown she made for the races. McKenna's sister is come to stay and learn the trade for 12 months. All doing well and getting good health. Herself ** and John Mc would have been at Tuam races only that two of the men went on duty to the

*Katie's sister
**Katie

North for the 12th of July where it was feared that disturbance would take place.

So John did not get to the races because he had to cover for men who were sent north for the Twelfth of July. He would later have direct experience of the Twelfth in Cookstown, Co. Tyrone. Before marrying John, Katie had been what was described as a 'scientific' dressmaker, by all accounts a good one. One of John's sisters from the farm in Annagap, Co. Monaghan stayed with him and Katie to learn the trade.

Katie was a strong-willed individual, who did not follow her sisters into the teaching profession, something encouraged by their mother who had been one of the first trained female teachers in Ireland. Although RIC regulations forbade the wives of policeman to earn money as dressmakers, she did not let this prevent her from practising unofficially. Her mother, corresponding with Katie's brother Laurence in 1896, referred to 'a young man of the RIC' telling him

> there is an engagement between himself and Katie and that she informed you of it and that you liked it. What truth there is in that I don't know, he seems to be a nice young man as far as I can see. He is a stranger to me except for the past few months, so you will kindly tell me what you think.

John and Katie would have 12 children, one of whom, Peter, (now deceased) was the father of the editor of this memoir. Another child, Florence, died at four years of age, while James, the eldest son, died aged 16 in the Spanish 'flu epidemic after the end of the Great War. Yet another child, Rose, died in infancy. Only one of John's children is alive at this time, Tony, now aged 91. Pauline lived until her 100th year, but sadly passed away on 16 February 2009, before this book was published.

Katie came from Co. Galway, where John met her while on his first RIC posting. Her own father, James Byrne, had also been a member of the RIC before retiring after 31 years. John's humble background as the second son of a farmer led to friction with his future bride's family, with Katie's eldest brother Laurence (then just recently qualified as a barrister) initially opposed to the union. A letter dated 26 September 1896 covered the relationship between Katie and her husband to be. It was written by James Byrne (Katie's father) to Laurence:

> Laurence I would do everything in my power to serve Katie but I will not undertake to be accountable for her actions. I think she ought to be capable of minding herself. I assure you I never knew of any engagement between Katie and the young man until he came and told Mother of it when Mother called and told me of it. I may say I was surprised but said nothing.
>
> The young man seems very affectionate and as far as I know has a good character in the Force. I would be averse to a stealthy marriage or elopement and the young man would not be entitled to get leave for 12 months to come or thereabouts. Katie may do as she thinks proper but this I would say, that things of that kind, viz breaking after making promise is in my opinion very reprehensible and does not turn out well. I had nothing to do with Mother's writing but I know she had no notion of compromising you in any way. Mother told him that you and Katie would do whatever she told you, and that everything would come out right yet. That is the substance of what she wrote.

When James wrote of John getting leave, he was referring to being granted leave by the RIC to get married. The regulations stipulated that a policeman had to serve seven years before being given permission by his superiors to get married. After another eighteen months (not twelve, as James estimates) John would have served his seven years and be free to marry. His marriage took place just three weeks after his seven years in the RIC had been served. As a former RIC man himself, James would have been aware of the force's regulations.

In a letter dated 30 September 1896, just four days after the one mentioned above, John wrote to his future brother-in-law Laurence Byrne, saying:

> Your Mother told me that you think Katie could do better. That I'm sure is true, but does wealth always bring happiness? Mine, I know, is a humble position, but it may be

better. There is no stain on my character, so that I may have
a chance to compete for promotion if I wish.

John would find promotion more difficult to achieve than he anticipated in his early days as a constable. But he would have the comfort of being cherished by Katie, as the same letter mentioned above made clear. John asked Laurence to show forbearance in the disagreement which arose between them over Katie:

If you could only imagine yourself to be in the same position as I am in and know how dearly I love Katie I'm sure you wouldn't be so hard on us.

It is worth noting that Laurence and John would later become good friends, and their respective families kept in touch through the years. Laurence and his descendants deserve credit for having preserved a considerable number of letters from the late-nineteenth and early-twentieth centuries, providing a remarkable insight into life at the time. All the letters were written to Laurence or his wife, whether by his father, mother, brothers or sisters, even occasionally his in-laws. The tranquil days in Galway ended when John requested, and got, a transfer to Ballymena in Co. Antrim. His appointment there started on 10 October 1903. The move north was mentioned by Katie's father to his son Laurence in a letter dated 22 October 1903:

I may tell you that we have had a letter from my dear daughter Katie, who is staying with her three children at McKenna's father's place in County Monaghan until McKenna gets settled in Ballymena Co. Antrim, where he has been transferred at his own request, having sold out all his furniture at Barna.

We see from the letters that Laurence was the decision maker in the Byrne family, the man to whom they all looked for guidance and support. Katie and Laurence's father, James, although still hale and hearty, was by this time a man in his seventies. His wife Sarah was younger, in her early sixties. Both parents wanted the best for all their children, and Katie seemed to have been especially loved by the entire family (seven children in total).

Difficulties for the young family would follow, and Katie was not taken with Ballymena from the outset, even though the house they lived in was spacious and well-appointed. In a letter from Sarah Byrne, Katie's mother, to Laurence, dated 09 March 1904, she said:

> I had a letter from Katie from Ballymena (a town she does not like) and she is anxious to get a photo of the group you sent me if Mary had one to spare.

For all that, Katie did her best to see something of the part of the country she now lived in. Another letter, this time from mother to son, dated 04 December 1904, mentioned the McKenna family:

> Katie and her family are all in good health. She went to see Portrush and the Giant's Causeway. She saw Scotland in the distance.

Ballymena would be the scene of almost unbearable grief for Katie when her four year old child Florence died. This came just after the death of her own mother Sarah back in Galway. In a letter dated 26 May 1905, Katie poured her heart out to Mary, Laurence's wife:

> Mary she was a lovely child, I wish now I had a good photograph of her ... It was very hard on me to lose our good kind mother, but it was harder still to lose little Florence, but ... we are sure at least, she is in Heaven.

Katie had by this time four children: Florence, James, Mary Jo and Peter. He was an infant child of nine months when the letter was written:

> My youngest child Henry Peter is, the doctors say, at present dangerously ill, he has an abscess on his right leg, which is very painful.

Although child mortality and illness was much greater one hundred years ago than it is today, this did not lessen the impact it had on parents of the time, who had to deal with such things along with the inevitable death of their own parents. Katie mentioned in the same letter the recent funeral of her own mother Sarah, only in her mid-sixties when she died:

> I was very sorry when John told me Laurence was late for mother's funeral, for I believe, could she have said so, she would wait for her loved eldest child.

Laurence was then living in England, and doubtless experienced greater difficulties in returning to the west of Ireland than would be the case today. This was the background to John's family life in Ballymena in 1905, and we can only imagine the toll it took on his emotional life and that of his young family.

> I ... sincerely hope, Mary, neither you nor Laurence will ever be called upon, as I have for the last two weeks, to watch my little darling dragged away, frantic with pain, and powerless to aid her in any way. Peritonitis she died of.

John was promoted to Acting Sergeant on 01 July 1907, something which was mentioned in passing by his father-in-law back in Galway when writing to John's brother-in-law, Laurence, in a letter dated 02 September 1907:

> I have not heard from McKenna recently but Sergeant O'Sullivan told me he was promoted.

A move for John to Carnlough, Co. Antrim in 1908 was followed by a transfer to Larne in 1914. Further postings were to Kenmare, Co. Kerry on 11 September 1920; Cookstown, Co. Tyrone on 1 November 1920; and Kildare on 1 August 1921, prior to disbandment at the Curragh.

The memoir is short, around 16,000 words, but is well-written and covers a period of momentous change in Ireland, north and south. It was written in 1932, 11 years after the latest events in John's RIC career mentioned in the memoir, and was triggered by the events in Larne in June of that year. These later events related to the Eucharistic Congress in Dublin, (an international Catholic religious event intended to renew and strengthen the faith) to which a party of Larne Catholics and others from the surrounding area travelled by boat from Larne Harbour. The sectarian attacks on these pilgrims as they processed to the boat from the local church were well-documented in the press of the time.

Also documented was the lack of resolve on the part of the Royal Ulster Constabulary (RUC), the successors to the Royal Irish Constabulary (RIC) in Northern Ireland, when it came to dealing with the Loyalist assaults. John did not join the RUC after the disbandment of the RIC in 1922, and was ten years retired in 1932. Policemen could retire on a full pension after 30 years service, which is what John did. He saw the way the police dealt with the disturbances in Larne as symptomatic of the Northern Ireland government's disregard for the rights of the politico-religious minority.

John's anger found expression in recounting the injustices he had experienced and observed in the years he served in the RIC in Counties Tyrone and Antrim. His experiences in the north contrasted sharply with more peaceful times in Galway and chronicled his awakening to the political and sectarian influences of the force he had joined.

His recollections of his experiences in Cookstown, Co. Tyrone in the 1920–21 period are particularly poignant, but they do not take into account the fact that there was an Irish Republican Army (IRA) attack on the barracks just 5 months before he was posted there. This would have coloured the perspective of the security forces personnel he found himself working with (for more details see the extended reports of this attack in the conclusion).

It is also important to remember that John's memories of his RIC career as recalled in 1932 were, in his opinion, 'somewhat ancient history'. This may include (for instance) remembering events as being closer together than they actually were. Yet much of what he wrote is borne out by contemporary press accounts, records and files in the public domain.

After being disbanded from the RIC in 1922, John McKenna went to work as manager of an estate in London for seven years, leaving his family behind in Larne. He returned in 1929 when his wife Katie passed away, his youngest child Tony having just turned eleven at the time. This prolonged absence may partly explain his disillusionment with the Northern Ireland state, considering he had only been back living in Larne for not quite three years when he penned the memoir.

His son Peter (born in 1904, he lived until he was eighty-six; the late father of the editor) believed that the absence was not wholly from choice, that 'he went over to London ... partly for security and fear of retaliation', a quote taken from Peter McKenna's own short memoir, 'A Song of Home'. Whatever the real reason for John's absence, it seems that his return was driven by the necessity of looking after his younger children after his beloved wife Katie died.

THE EUCHARISTIC
CONGRESS 1932

Author's Original
Preface

Larne 7th July, 1932

The very cowardly attack on us pilgrims who were proceeding on 26th ult. from the Church of St MacNissi to Larne Harbour where we were to embark for Dublin on the S.S. Princess Margaret has spurred me on to do that which I have been thinking of doing for a long time i'e, write some of my experiences in the RIC but before beginning to describe what is now somewhat ancient history I may as well give an account of this brutal cowardly and altogether unprovoked attack on the pilgrims

About the beginning of February of this year in response to the advice of the local priest some 600 or 700 persons from Larne parish gave their names to the Secretary of the Committee which had been appointed in connection with the Eucharistic Congress, as intending pilgrims and in order to secure travelling accommodation for them Father H McGuigan C C communicated

John McKenna finally puts pen to paper. The present (1932) leads to the past, and helps him 'to write some of my experiences in the RIC', as mentioned in line 7 above.

The Eucharistic Congress 1932

Larne 7th July 1932

The very cowardly attack on us pilgrims who were proceeding on the 26th ult. [of that month: i.e. 26th June] from the Church of St. MacNissi to Larne Harbour, where we were to embark for Dublin on the *SS Princess Margaret*, has spurred me on to do that which I have been thinking of doing for a long time, i.e. write some of my experiences in the RIC. But before beginning what is now somewhat ancient history, I may as well give an account of this cowardly, brutal and altogether unprovoked attack on the pilgrims.

About the beginning of February of this year, in response to the advice of the local priest, some 600 or 700 persons from Larne Parish gave their names to the Secretary of the Committee (which had been appointed in connection with the Eucharistic Congress) as intending pilgrims. In order to secure accommodation for them, Father McGuigan CC communicated with Mr Getty of the LMS (London Midland & Scottish) Railway, Belfast, with a view to securing a special train for the Larne pilgrims.

Mr Getty replied, saying that they (the LMS) had already arranged for so many special trains for that day, 26th June, that it would be impossible to give one to us. He suggested that we should take their ship, the *Princess Victoria*[1], which would be idle in Larne Harbour on that date. I mention this fact here for the purpose of showing that the idea of going by sea was first suggested by the LMS and not by us, as some of the Belfast papers have commented on the novel way of travelling adopted by the Larne Parish. The Committee agreed to take the ship as suggested, but asked that the larger vessel, the *Princess Margaret*, would be sent.

Eventually, after much correspondence as well as interviews, the LMS agreed to send the larger vessel. The fares were fixed at 10/6 [ten shillings and sixpence] for the return journey, and tickets were sent to us to sell. When it was learnt that a ship was going from Larne, applications were received from Belfast, Carrickfergus, the Glens of Antrim and other surrounding parishes, so that in all over 1,200 availed themselves of that means of proceeding to the Congress.

Some weeks before the Congress, it was announced that, for the convenience of the pilgrims, there would be Midnight Mass in the Church of St MacNissi [Larne], and that immediately after Mass the pilgrims, accompanied by the two priests who were to go with them, would proceed to the ship in a body.

Having been appointed treasurer I had to attend at the McKenna Memorial School[2] on Sundays after Mass, and on Wednesday and Friday evenings for some weeks for the purpose of receiving funds and issuing tickets. As I was going to the school on the 24th ult. [June 1932] the Head Constable stopped me and asked if I was going to Dublin. I said yes. He then asked me to try and stop the 'marching', as he called our going in a body to the boat, saying there was a very bad feeling about it in the town. I said to him why should there be. There is nothing political in our going to Dublin and we will give offence to no person, and besides, I added, every person who is not going should be in their beds at that hour. To which he replied, 'Oh God no, on Saturday night there will be hundreds[3] out at that time. There is a very bad feeling, so try and throw oil on troubled waters.'

I may say here that I had been on duty on Saturday nights in Larne for over six years and I never saw crowds of hundreds or even dozens on the streets after midnight. I told him I would mention the matter when I got to the school, and I did so, but found that they (the Committee) knew all about what the Head Constable had told me as he had been in communication with Father [Bernard] McLaverty. He, as a mere matter of courtesy, had written to advise the District Inspector that we were going at 1.30 am.

The Committee, most of whom were reared in Larne, only laughed at the idea of an attack being made on us, and from my experience of Larne I confess that I did not think there would be, but we were soon to learn otherwise.

At Midnight Mass the Church was packed. I was there, and as a member of the Committee assisted in finding seats for the pilgrims who arrived from surrounding parishes. After Mass the congregation was addressed by Father McLaverty CC, who told the pilgrims to assemble together after Mass, and that in a short time he and Father Kelly would accompany them to the Harbour. He advised them against doing or saying anything which would give offence to any person, and as far as I saw or heard, his advice was strictly observed.

As soon as the priests came we proceeded towards the Harbour in the following order: 1st cross bearer, Mr John Loughrey carried the cross, the recognised symbol of Christianity. He was followed by the priests, after whom came the women pilgrims, the choir, and last the men pilgrims, two of whom carried a small Eucharistic banner. When we got to the War Memorial, there was a noisy crowd of about 100[4] or more persons lined up with some police in front of them. But with the exception of the usual vulgar and offensive expressions, jeering and singing, nothing in the shape of violence took place until we got to the Aluminium Works.

Here, shower after shower of stones and other missiles began to come upon us from the railway line, cutting and wounding a number. I did not see a policeman from the time we passed the Memorial until we got to the Harbour. I saw some police at the Harbour, but even then, as we passed along over the rails between the station and the coalsheds, showers of stones were thrown.

Inside the Harbour station, not far from the steerage gangway, there was a crowd of about 50 singing and shouting offensive epithets as the pilgrims got on board. After some time some police came and put this crowd back a distance from the boat and the singing and shouting ceased for a short time. It was then that the men's portion of the pilgrims began to arrive, and as the man who was carrying the banner poles went to go on the gangway, I saw a man get hold of one of the poles and break it.

Immediately a policeman came and took the man away from the gangway. As he was doing this I said to him, 'that man is after breaking that pole.' I thought at the time that the policeman took the man into custody, but learned afterwards that he did not do so.

As the boat left the quay another shower of stones came on board, accompanied by the usual singing and vulgar epithets. Such was our send off to the great Eucharistic Congress from this supposedly civilised town of Larne, Ireland. When we got to a safe distance from the shore and had a look around us for victims of the onslaught, it was found that a goodly number were getting their heads bandaged.

In the Phoenix Park, when some of us wandered away from our section before the High Mass, those bandaged heads, particularly one of a very tall man from Carnlough, proved useful to us finding our way back to our allotted ground. There were no other bandaged heads in the vicinity, so we soon found our places by making for the spot where the bandaged heads were to be seen.

Since writing the foregoing I have seen the correspondence between our beloved Bishop and Sir Dawson Bates regarding this attack – it was published in the *Irish News*. It was only what I had expected and had told some of my fellow pilgrims on the boat. There was not even one name taken by the police and they saw nothing wrong being done. They are in fact highly commended for the manner in which they did their duty.

Of course they did their duty – the duty their employers expected of them. They protected the people who pelted us in case any of us would strike back. Even the man who took the banner pole, and who was apparently taken into custody, was neither arrested or charged. He was working for the LMS that night and is, I understand, still employed by the company. I do not know the man personally, but I am glad that neither he nor the other poor hungry dupes who were employed to stone us are being punished.

It is their employers (many of whom are now acting the hypocrite in condemning the attack) that I would like to see punished and not their unfortunate dupes. But it is better still that none are to be even summonsed, as the tribunal before whom they appear might, like the wolf who accused the lamb of disturbing the wolves' waters from which it was drinking, decide that it was we, legally and quietly proceeding to the boat, who were the aggressors on the occasion and not they.

However, enough about the incident. It was, after all, only a trivial affair in comparison with some of the scenes I witnessed in 1921 and the preceding years. It was only the Catholics of Larne who were astonished, as unlike other towns in the Six Counties, Larne was fortunate in having, during the changeover from the British Government to the Orangemen, an honest man as a District Inspector. They thus escaped the gruelling the Catholics in other places had to endure.

I have never met him (Mr. Barrington), but before and after coming to Larne I have often heard him spoken of as an honest, straight man. The fact that he was successful in keeping the Specials in Larne from committing anything like the outrages which I saw convinced me that what I heard about him was true. How different my own life, and that of many Catholic civilians, would have been had other men of his rank acted as he did.

Notes

1. This was the ship which perished with terrible loss of life in the North Channel in 1953.

2. This was the National, later Primary, School which was built in 1898 and dedicated to the memory of the recently deceased Parish Priest, Francis McKenna – no relation to John McKenna or any of his family. John's oldest son James was a monitor (a kind of prefect with a supervisory role) at McKenna Memorial at the time of his death (aged 16) in 1918. He was one of the casualties of the Spanish 'flu epidemic just after the end of the Great War. The school was demolished in the mid-1970's after the opening of St Joseph's Primary at the beginning of that decade.

3. Although the Head Constable in Larne at the time may have had his finger on the pulse of the Protestant community, it is hard to see how McKenna could have 'poured oil on troubled waters' – it was maybe unrealistic for the RUC to expect the procession to be cancelled. Some form of procession or convoy would have been necessary to take the large gathering of Catholics the mile or so to the Harbour from the Church.

Father Bernard McLaverty, one of the priests accompanying the procession to the Harbour, wrote a letter to the RUC responding to their appeal to stop the procession. It was dated 24 June 1932:

Dear Sir,

I thank you for your communication of yesterday. The committee in charge, including myself, cannot see the necessity of changing our arrangements, namely that the congregation of 900 or so, after Mass in St MacNissi's Church will proceed in due order to the steamer at Larne Harbour. I think you overestimate the importance of such an event and the magnitude of the task of protection. You do not need to protect the whole route but the procession.

No colours will be worn as the procession is entirely religious: the colours will be worn on the hearts of the people. Of course the procession will be headed by a crossbearer and also a Eucharistic Congress banner will be carried.

Again I thank you for your trouble in this matter.

Yours sincerely,
Father McLaverty

Father McLaverty gave a sermon in St MacNissi's Church in Larne the week before the Congress in which he hailed the event in Dublin as heralding the triumph of Catholic Ireland over all adversities. The sermon featured prominently in the *Irish News* of 21 June 1932, and mentioned such keynote events in Irish history as the Penal Laws and Cromwell. The *Irish News* article is worth quoting in full, as it gives us an idea of the mindset of the Catholics in Larne (or at least one of their priests) in the days leading up to the Congress.

TRIUMPH OF CATHOLIC IRELAND

Larne Priest on Significance of the Congress

The Rev. B. McLaverty, C.C., preaching in St MacNissi's Church, Larne, on the significance of the Congress, said it signified a great triumph – the triumph of Catholic Ireland over 750 years of persecution such as even the early Romans or the Jews had not endured.

It was small wonder, he declared, that Mr Hillaire Belloc, the great Catholic writer, had described the preservation of the Faith by the Irish people as an historical miracle comparable to nothing else in Europe's history.

When Cromwell landed in Ireland he marched through the country with a Bible in one hand and the sword in the other, and boasted that he would either drive the Catholics to Hades or Connaught, and as part of his wicked scheme, cut down Irish peasants and their only means of livelihood. But they still had Catholic Connaught as the figurative of Catholic Ireland, and there was no Cromwell.

> In the wider context of Loyalist Larne, this may not have gone down too well with the rougher element that would be out in the early hours of the following Sunday morning. The heading itself would have been enough to provoke their ire, fuelling the idea that the procession itself was a triumphalist one.
>
> The extensive reports on the Congress in the *Irish News* editions of the time speak of unquestioning loyalty to the Church and its interpretation of Irish history, and the sensitivities of Ulster Loyalists were not considered. This was shown by the jocular references in the paper to Loyalists erecting arches and bunting in honour of the Congress. In turn this reflected the buoyant mood prevailing in the Catholic north in the weeks before the event in Dublin. That the Twelfth was not too far off was somehow disregarded.

McKenna's life was enmeshed with the Church, and his unquestioning devotion to 'our beloved Bishop' and Catholic rituals would have not been unusual in those days, unbelievable as this may now seem to a more sceptical generation living in the wake of numerous Church scandals. Prior to partition, the Church had consistently opposed revolutionary violence. After partition, while McKenna's devotion to his religion continued, the Church was less concerned with the political aspirations of their flock than with control of Catholic education. The denial of full grants to Catholic (voluntary) schools was a major grievance among nationalists and the hierarchy alike.

McKenna was a man who had served the British State faithfully in the belief that Ireland would remain undivided under the Crown, with powers devolved to the whole country under Home Rule. As a devout Catholic, his British-Irish identity foundered in a Unionist-dominated state which did not recognise his religion as being compatible with Britishness. This was the significance of the Congress, given the Loyalist reaction to it, in McKenna's life.

It was likely the Catholics from Larne and the surrounding areas would have anticipated some reaction from their Loyalist neighbours, but the newspaper reports of the time suggest that a kind of holy invincibility prevailed. In Larne, in the aftermath of the Congress, the RUC suggested that some Catholics had changed their plans by making their own way to the steamer, i.e. by not taking part in the procession. A statement from the RUC Inspector General's Office said that 'at least 500 persons took the advice of police and boarded the steamer early in their own time.' It is possible that there being no room for all the pilgrims in the Larne church was the reason for going directly to the steamer.

4. An *Irish News* report of the time implied that 'hundreds' of sullen Loyalist observers were lining the street immediately outside the Church as the congregation emerged and the procession began. This may have been untrue, as McKenna, or other witnesses whose testimony was reported at the time, would have mentioned this had it been the case. The first hostile crowds were assembled at the Cenotaph, a few hundred yards round the corner from the Church. It was also (correctly) reported that buses carrying elderly and disabled people ahead of the procession were stoned, with their windows being broken.

The Statement from the RUC Inspector General's Office said that

> a crowd of about 700 had assembled between the Jetty and the Railway Crossing. About 400 people at the Railway Crossing were very hostile, and the police drove this party back towards the Olderfleet Hotel ...two buses crossed the Bridge near the Olderfleet Hotel. These buses should have proceeded by a different route ... they arrived in the centre of a hostile crowd of about 200 persons.

In a letter to the *Irish News*, Bishop Mageean (of the Diocese of Down and Connor) denied that the Curate, Father Bernard McLaverty, had given any undertaking or had reached any agreement with the police to take a particular route. This is crucial, as the police used this as the reason why they were unable to protect the buses. The Bishop also pointed out that the buses were not part of the procession, as they arrived at the Harbour well ahead of it – his response to the assertion that the Loyalists were only attacking the procession, not individuals as such.

Cars coming away from the harbour with Catholics who were seeing people off were also attacked. A rumour that the convent grounds were about to be stormed from the Curran Road by disgruntled Loyalists in the aftermath of the ship's departure proved to be false, as acknowledged by the *Irish News*.

In a letter to the *Irish News* on 07 July 1932, Father McLaverty stated that only 150 were in the mob on the pier, and suggested that the police should have been able to deal effectively with such a number. The *Irish News* editorial of 01 July 1932 supported the belief that the police did not do enough to prevent violence, as

... we are assured from more than one hand that the presence of ten or twelve police – determined on maintaining law and order – at and around the Harbour gates at Larne would have prevented most, if not all, of the shameful scenes that occurred there. Why were they not there?

In correspondence between the Bishop and Dawson Bates, the Minister for Home Affairs, published in the *Irish News* (the same correspondence referred to by McKenna in his memoir) the Minister's Assistant Secretary asserted that four sergeants and 17 constables were specially drafted into Larne to deal with the situation. 'If the police had been told that the clergy intended to march at the head of the procession in their vestments the Minister is informed that they would not have allowed the procession to proceed, as this was calculated to lead to a breach of the peace, and is, in addition, contrary to law, as your Lordship is no doubt aware.' This letter was dated 01 July 1932.

Bishop Mageean, while responding to other points raised in the letter, did not address this one. Did this imply an admission that the priests McLaverty and Kelly (the latter from Glenarm Parish) were unwise wearing their vestments at the head of the procession? Were they aware of the crowds on the streets? Was it realistic of the RUC to blame the Catholics for provoking Loyalists at one o'clock on a Sunday morning, at a time when all those not travelling to Dublin should have been in bed, as McKenna suggested in his memoir? In Larne, Loyalists stayed up into the small hours to vent their anger.

An RUC suggestion that by 'making their own way' to the steamer the Catholics would have ensured they would not have been attacked may have been misleading. If the overall total of around 1,400 people (assuming the police estimate of 500 making their own way to the steamer, and Fr. McLaverty's figure of 900 in the Church congregation are both correct – McKenna put the figure travelling to Dublin at around 1,200) had decided not to attend Mass and make their own way to the harbour, it seemed likely that an attack would still have been mounted.

It is difficult to imagine that some form of Loyalist response would not have been forthcoming, given incidents in numerous other Loyalist towns in the north where pilgrims were also attacked. Having said that, it was not uncommon (judging by the notices in the *Irish News* in the period leading up to the Congress) for pilgrims to assemble in a body and process to the relevant train or bus station, although not in such an overtly religious manner as they did in Larne. Doubtless the pilgrims in places such as Belfast or Ballymena considered there was safety in numbers, and we have no way of telling today what the Loyalist response in Larne would have been had no processions at all taken place. The nature of the Eucharistic Congress, considering the fervour of priests and people, meant that no procession of any kind taking place would have been extremely unlikely.

Apart from the attack on the procession and the two buses, windows were broken in the Catholic Church and McKenna Memorial School, and Catholic businesses such as Francis Donnelly's on the Old Glenarm Road were attacked.

The *Larne Times and Weekly Telegraph* did not give the trouble surrounding the departure of the Catholics from Larne Harbour much prominence, although a curious report in the edition dated 02 July 1932 was headlined:

LARNE CATHOLICS AND CONGRESS
THE VISIT TO DUBLIN
A SUCCESSFUL EVENT
(Contributed)

The article may have been 'contributed' by someone who was told not to mention the attack, and had the tenor of a parish report describing the activities of the priests, with congratulations offered to both them and the organising committee. Here is one of the closing paragraphs:

> Immediately after the service the pilgrims assembled in Agnew Street, the vicinity being thronged with spectators, and to the strains of the rousing old hymn, "Faith of Our Fathers," marched in procession to the harbour. The procession was led by a cross-bearer, Mr J Loughrey, a local student in the Passionist Order, followed by the Rev. Father McLaverty and Rev. Father Kelly. A beautiful silk and gold

embroidered Eucharistic banner was also carried by one of the pilgrims.

No mention at all was made in this report of the stoning and abuse of the Congress pilgrims which took place, and the only reference which could be found to it in the 02 July edition was buried away in a column relating to activity in the Magistrate's Court:

BENCH AND ROWDY CONDUCT

Before the ordinary business of the court was begun the Chairman said he had been asked to make the following announcement:- "The magistrates of Larne Petty Sessions district most sincerely deplore the breach of the peace which took place on Sunday morning, and wish to assure the public that they (the magistrates) will do their part in bringing the perpetrators to justice."

The omission of any serious reporting on the disturbances is puzzling. The edition of the 09 July *Larne Times and Weekly Telegraph* again gave scant coverage, with sub-headings under Larne Urban Council including 'Malicious Injury Claims' and 'Aftermath of Harbour Scenes'.

The malicious injury claims were described under the heading:

HOOLIGANISM

The Town Clerk reported that arising out of the disturbances at Larne Harbour on the night of June 25, he had received malicious injury compensation claims totalling £242 6s. The separate items were:- Miss Eileen McErlean, 91 Old Glenarm Road, Larne, personal injuries £200; Trustees of Roman Catholic Church, Larne, windows broken, £11; Francis Erwin, Cullybackey Road, Ballymena, damages to motor car, £5; L M & S Railway Co. damages to buses, £20 18s; Francis Donnelly, 60 Old Glenarm Road, Larne, windows broken and damaged, £5 8s.

Mr McConnell:- That was the worst bit of hooliganism I have heard of in the town. It was a disgrace that "bits of boys " should be allowed to carry on like that.

Mr Jenkins:- No doubt about that.

It was resolved to refer the claims to the Council's solicitor, with authority to engage what professional assistance be needed for the defence.

This was the full report, and the only real acknowledgement in the paper that Loyalists attacked Congress pilgrims in Larne during the early hours of June 26 1932.

Another contemporary's account of the Congress was written by Edward O'Toole in the 1970's. Edward was the Purser on the *Princess Margaret*, and he recollected the febrile atmosphere in Larne in the weeks leading up to the journey. The painted kerbstones, the banners and flags, along with the taunting of Catholics in the workplace were mentioned. He recalled the pilgrims on their way to Church that night, excitedly wondering what would await them when they walked to the boat afterwards. The details of the pilgrims being showered with coal and stones were verified, with the attackers taking cover behind coal wagons at the railway sidings on the approach to the Harbour.

Edward stated that he, John McKenna and the two priests leading the East Antrim pilgrims, went by jaunting car upon arrival in Dublin to the Phoenix Park. There they went to the Press Bureau, apparently situated under the main altar, where they reported the events in Larne to the media. They in turn duly spread the news of this and other sectarian attacks in the north related to the Congress. Also mentioned was a certain coolness by Larne Loyalists towards their Catholic neighbours in the aftermath of the Congress, along with an unofficial boycott of Catholic businesses in the town.

The *Irish News* of 10 August 1932 stated in an editorial that the total number of RUC personnel on duty in the early hours of Sunday 26 June was 19 constables, four sergeants, a Head Constable and the District Inspector. At the Court sitting in Larne on the events of that night, the Head Constable went

into the witness box to give identification evidence intended to exonerate certain "B" Specials who were among the suspects in the dock, although neither he nor any other policeman would swear evidence against a single defendant ...

The Head Constable's plea to McKenna to stop the procession is put into perspective in the light of his refusal to testify against either the Specials or any Loyalists. From the outset, the pilgrims were portrayed by the police as being the only troublemakers.

The Court's findings were that no case was proven against the accused and the *Irish News* decried the fact that no policeman gave evidence against any of the defendants, despite being present when the attacks were carried out. Neither were any arrests made on the night.

The *Irish News* also noted:

the conspicuous lack of any comment from the magistrates about this slur on the honour of their town. Rather we would refer to the one vital confession made by District Inspector Martin, who suggested the disturbances had their inspiration in the visit to the town made by a certain Protestant preacher.

> The *Newsletter* (the main Unionist paper) of the same date suggested that off duty 'B' Specials were on the streets that night trying to keep order. It also suggested that pilgrims in the procession shouted 'Up Dublin' and 'Up De Valera' in response to taunting and abuse from Loyalists at the Cenotaph, who sang 'Dolly's Brae'. In response by a plea from a woman pilgrim to let them 'have their day', a Special and an associate allegedly burst into 'The Sash'. The paper mentioned that pilgrims sang hymns for the duration of the procession.
>
> The *Belfast Telegraph* of 27 June 1932 reported the actual events of the Congress in Dublin in quite respectful tones. As for the events in Larne, they were described under the sub-heading of

STONE THROWING AT LARNE

After Mass at the Larne church, a procession was formed, headed by three surpliced clergymen, one of whom carried a large golden cross, and the pilgrims marched to the harbour singing Congress hymns. Unfortunately on the way there were some stone throwing incidents from bands of irresponsible youths among the hundreds of spectators and the windows of a couple of buses conveying the older people to the steamer were smashed.

A large body of police on duty under D.I. Martin averted more serious consequences and although there was a recurrence of long range stone throwing at the harbour, there were only one or two very minor injuries.

> This article said that over 1,200 passengers sailed on the *Princess Margaret* to Dublin under the Captain, Andrew Hamilton.
>
> The assault on the pilgrims in Larne was also reported in the *Irish Times*, which was the main paper still representing southern unionist opinion after partition.
>
> In the edition dated Monday 27 June, the events in Larne were headlined:

STEAMER PILGRIMS
PASS THROUGH FUSILADE OF STONES

Pilgrims en route to the Eucharistic Congress in Dublin were attacked by a mob while marching to board a steamer at Larne.

Two omnibuses, carrying elderly people from a Roman Catholic Church Service arrived at the steamer with nothing but the window frames on one side of the bus, while some of the passengers had cuts on their faces.

The main procession of pilgrims was pelted on the way to the quay, several people being struck by the stones.

Two motor cars, one of them with a priest as passenger, went through a fusilade of stones.

An attempt was made to rush the gangway.

An attempt to snatch a Eucharistic banner from its bearer was checked by the police, but was followed by stone throwing at the steamer.

Women took shelter behind the bulwarks. One or two men received nasty blows on the face.

Windows and portholes on the steamer were broken, and even as the vessel steamed out volley after volley of stones land upon her decks.

> The differing emphasis on the reporting of the events relating to the Congress in Larne reflected the priorities of the various newspapers' readership, but it is difficult to imagine the RUC in 1932 Larne treating Loyalists any differently than did their RIC predecessors at the time of the gun-running in April 1914.

A Beleaguered Station

A Memoir

call another meeting but the other said no, there was no use - they would never form a branch of the Ulster Volunteers in Carnlough. I returned to the barracks & reported that there were no Ulster Volunteers in Carnlough, that a meeting for the purpose of forming a branch attended by 28 persons including some old men & some small boys was held in the Town Hall on that date, and that the meeting broke up after about 10 minutes without forming a branch. This report was quite true but I soon found out that it wasn't a true report they wanted. It was very necessary to frighten as quickly them with the size of the Ulster volunteer army which was going to march to Cork in the event of the Home Rule Bill coming into operation. In about a week after this report of mine, the arms were landed in Larne. This same D.I. was walking about the Harbour that night smoking and the County Inspectors motor cars was there conveying the arms to their destination & in about a month because of my truthful report I was transferred to Larne. This transfer ruined me. I had eight small children - one only a fortnight.

McKenna recalls the transfer from Carnlough to Larne which he thought was against RIC regulations. On a personal level he believed the 'transfer ruined me', as mentioned at the bottom of the page.

Halcyon Days in the West: Galway to Carnlough

IN THE YEAR 1891, TO BE EXACT THE 2ND OF MARCH, I joined the RIC in the twentieth year of my existence. As I was the second son of a small farmer who had nothing to spare of this world's goods, I thought myself very lucky, as it was then considered both an honourable and even affluent position for a country boy. After the usual period of training I was sent to Galway, where I spent the first twelve years of my service. Very, very often I have regretted since that I ever asked to leave the west. During those twelve years I was happy, except for the tyranny of some of the District Inspectors I met, but as far as the inhabitants were concerned, I found nothing but the height of civility and friendship.

As for police duty, there was really nothing to be done except to summons a man for being drunk at a fair, or a farmer for occasionally allowing his pig or dog to walk on the road. An ambitious policeman thought himself lucky when he found an ass or pig on the road, as it meant 'a case' opposite his name in the monthly summary prosecutions which had to be prepared for the inspecting officers. A man who did not have a few prosecutions after his name was not considered energetic. I must not have been considered energetic then, or at least a drunken officer once told me so, and threatened that if I did not improve I would get no privileges, leave etc. I told him I would not make cases where they didn't occur, but from what I knew of him afterwards, I think he thought I should.

However, I got away from his district and after a short time came to County Antrim and was stationed in Ballymena. Before leaving Galway I had been examined for promotion by the County Inspector, a Mr Lopdell – the only real gentleman I ever met of his rank, and was placed on what was called the seniority list of candidates fit for promotion. According to the regulations, my name should have been put on the promotion list in Co. Antrim when I arrived there, but after what we called a general inspection by a Headquarters officer from Dublin, I found I was not on the list and applied to know why.

My appeal went through to Galway where the CI gave me an excellent character and stated that I held a high place on his promotion list. The Antrim CI stated on returning my appeal that my name would be put on his list the following year if I was recommended by my officer.

In Ballymena a policeman's life was very different from that in Galway. I soon found there was no need to 'manufacture' cases. In fact I used to try and avoid making them sometimes, but it was impossible to avoid making almost daily arrests for drunkenness and disorderly conduct, etc. I always had plenty of cases. But to my surprise, when another general inspection came round, I was not on the promotion list. After two years' strenuous work my officer did not recommend me.

It was then I discovered that my religion was the obstacle. I knew that there was a competitive exam held yearly in Dublin by the Civil Service Commission, who would not know the religion of candidates. 30 places (promotions) would be given to the candidates who got the highest marks. I made a resolution that I would try and get on this list, which was known as the 'P' list.

The inspection at which I discovered that I was not on the promotion list was held in the month of April 1906. The following November I went up to Dublin for the 'P' exam, where, not withstanding [the fact] that there were 100 competitors, I was successful in getting the 19th place. I was promoted the following June, long before some of the men who were on patronage lists of the District Inspector (DI) and County Inspector (CI). In addition to securing promotion immediately – I had taken over two-thirds of the marks in the Civil Service exam – I was qualified for the highest rank in the Service as far as qualifications were concerned.

In 1907 I obtained at an exam in Dublin the Board of Trade certificate as Inspector of Weights and Measures. In 1908 I went in charge of Carnlough, a lovely station on the Antrim coast. Unlike Ballymena, Carnlough was more or less a Catholic village, or at least the Catholics were in the majority. As most of the non-Catholics were intermarried with Catholic families there were no religious disturbances. I was always able to deal with any ordinary crime that did occur there to the entire satisfaction of the inhabitants and my superiors. I was as happy after spending six years there as it was possible for anyone in my humble station in life (with a family of eight small children) to be.

As stated before, I was giving entire satisfaction to everyone, so I got the surprise of my life one morning in June 1914 on opening the official letters to find that, without warning and quite contrary to the regulations of the service, I was transferred to Larne. Prior to this time (1914) I knew, of course, that I was dealing with superiors who were bigots as far as conferring any favours or promotion were concerned.

I knew that, but for having won my promotions at the competitive exam, I would never have been advanced, but I did not dream that they were political partisans. No person in the RIC was to have any politics, according to the code, and if any man of any rank was proved to have taken part in politics he was to be severely punished or dismissed.

The Home Rule controversy was at its height during the three or four years before 1914; Unionist Clubs and Ulster Volunteers were on everybody's lips[1]. All men in charge of stations had to make what was known as 'the monthly confidential report' as to the state of his sub-district. In it, he had to state the name and number of every secret society, the number of members and whether they were active or dangerous to the state. The absence of any such societies or organisations was a testimonial to the efficiency of the police.

I had been reporting month after month during these years that I had no Unionist Clubs, no Ulster Volunteers. Innocently enough, I was congratulating myself on the fact that my sub-district was free from these organisations, when to my surprise the District Inspector[2] officer inspecting the station one month early in 1914 asked me if I were quite sure that there were no Ulster Volunteers in my sub-district. I said yes.

He said that it was strange they were plentiful in all the other sub-districts. I explained to him that the few Protestant families we had were so intermarried with Catholics that it was impossible for them to get up to anything of the kind. Still he was not satisfied, and suggested the appointment of the only Protestant constable in the station as a special man to make enquiry and report, as he thought, owing to my religion, I might not be getting the right information. I said that I did not mind his appointing any man but asserted my information was right. He then asked [me] to go out to the day room and send in to him this constable.

In a few days time this constable handed me a sealed envelope addressed to the DI. I passed this letter on (and another some days later) without opening it, but when he handed me the third I opened it in his presence. I told him I would receive no more sealed reports from him, but if he had anything to report he would hand it to me so that I could, in compliance with the regulations, read and submit it in the ordinary way.

In this letter I found that he was reporting that there were 100 Ulster Volunteers in the sub-district. In a few days time a pass order, asking for a report of the number of Unionist Clubs, Ulster Volunteers, branches of the Irish League, etc., came by post signed by the Head Constable (a Catholic); the DI was sick. The order had to be noted for compliance and passed to Cushendall, so I asked this Constable to supply me with the information regarding the Volunteers, etc. He wanted to keep the official order, and when I pointed out that I had to send it to Cushendall, he said he couldn't give the information until after a meeting which was to be held in the town hall at 7 pm that evening.

This meeting, which I had reason to know had been got up by the Constable himself, was no secret to me. I had heard it was to be held, so I told the Constable not to trouble about the meeting, as I would find all the required information myself. I went that evening to the town hall at about 6.50 pm and stood beside the door talking to two men, James Dunlop and Charles Bamford, both Protestants. While I was speaking to them a number of men and boys, 28 altogether, went up the stairs to the town hall.

Dunlop was in charge of a store which was under the hall, and as the night was cold he opened the door and said we might as well go in out of the cold. We could hear the noise of the men moving over our heads in the hall, and Dunlop, who knew why they were there quite well, tried to draw me to know how much I knew by saying, 'I wonder what they are up to tonight', but knowing what he wanted I said I did not know.

To my surprise, and his, they began to come down the stairs again in about ten minutes. As they were coming down the stairs Dunlop slammed the door of the coal shed to, saying, 'we won't let them see us.' He really wanted to prevent me seeing who was at the meeting, but in reality he couldn't have helped me better in getting the information I required, as the two leading men stood outside the door within a foot of where I was and discussed their failure to form a branch of the Ulster Volunteers in Carnlough. One of them said they would call another meeting, but the other said no, there was no use, they would never form a branch of the Ulster Volunteers in Carnlough.

I returned to the barracks and reported that there were no Ulster Volunteers in Carnlough, that a meeting to propose the forming of a branch was attended by 28 persons, including some old men and small boys, was held in the town hall and broke up after about ten minutes without forming a branch. This report was quite true, but I found out that it wasn't a true report they wanted. It was very necessary to frighten Asquith then with the size of the Ulster Volunteers' army which was going to march to Cork in the event of Home Rule coming into operation.

In about a week after this report of mine the arms were landed in Larne.[3] This same District Inspector was walking about the Harbour that night smoking, and the County Inspector's motor car was there conveying arms to their destination. In about a month, because of my truthful report, I was transferred to Larne. This transfer ruined me.

Notes

1. One of Dublin Castle's moles at this time in the Ulster Unionist Council believed that a section of the Unionist leadership wanted to avoid confrontation with the Government. The mole, an RIC Sergeant, Joseph Edwards, reported on a debate in 1913 as to whether Unionists should be armed as 'Clubmen or Orangemen', but said a majority at the meeting were against the purchase of arms.

2. Paul Bew says that 'when the district inspectors and county inspectors [of the RIC] were asked to provide a wider overview they stressed rather a growing mood of loyalist intransigence.' In the Report of the Commissioners of Police (Belfast 1913), it was considered that prominent businessmen in the city who 'are less enthusiastic at present will be forced to take a more energetic part in the movement.' The County Inspector for Antrim said that 'any businessman who held back would be a marked man and his business would be ruined.'

Sir James Brown Dougherty, the Under Secretary to Augustine Birrell, the Chief Secretary for Ireland and himself a northern Presbyterian Home Ruler, considered such police reports to be exaggerated. On 13 March 1913 he told Birrell that

> DI's and CI's are lending themselves as willing instruments in a game of bluff ... it is perhaps necessary to remember that these officers are more closely associated with Unionist politicians and with the better classes in Ulster than they are with the masses.

The 1911 Census for Carnlough (for which McKenna acted as enumerator for much of the village, including his family and a separate return for the RIC) indicated three policemen serving in the village, including McKenna as Sergeant, along with two Constables. One of the Constables was listed as an Irish speaking Roman Catholic from Co. Roscommon, the other a member of the Church of Ireland from Co. Cavan. The latter was presumably the 'only Protestant' stationed in the Barracks who was used by the District Inspector, as he claimed, to get a more accurate picture of Ulster Volunteer activity in the village.

3. The smuggling of arms into Larne in April 1914 aboard the *Mountjoy*, later known as the *Clyde Valley*. It was remarkable for the extent to which the authorities turned a blind eye to what was taking place. This was the climax to the Loyalist hostility towards the Liberals' Third Home Rule Bill, a movement which McKenna saw as being orchestrated by elements of the establishment, including the British ruling classes in England and the higher echelons of the RIC.

The *Irish News* of Monday 27 April 1914 mentioned in an editorial that:

... 40,000, or 50,000, or 70,000 rifles were landed-they were not "smuggled", but landed in the harbours of populous towns while the King's servants were held prisoners by "superior forces" – in defiance of the Law and the Government in Larne, Bangor, and Donaghadee, on Friday night and Saturday morning.

The gun-running elsewhere in the same edition was covered in an article which emphasised the self-conscious history making indulged in by the Loyalists:

"THE GUN-RUNNERS"
Provisional Government's Coup at Larne.

The Ulster volunteers are pluming themselves on having brought off an historic coup when ... three consignments ... were put ashore at Bangor, Donaghadee, and Larne ... The poor fellows who donned their puttees and bandoliers and spent the night in wholly unnecessary vigils throughout all parts of the province have been unduly impressed now with the idea that they all shared in a most momentous and epoch making piece of strategy. Grossly exaggerated accounts have been sent far and wide as to the size and character of the importation, which was the central incident of the elaborate nocturnal "mobilisation": and the rank and file are being deluded into the belief that a shattering blow has been dealt at the Government and its policy ...

> The tendency to exaggerate must have been a trait Nationalists assumed Loyalists indulged in, and the *Irish News*' assumption that this was going on backs up McKenna's belief that something similar had been attempted in Carnlough regarding the true number of Ulster Volunteers in the village.
> The *Newsletter* of Saturday 25 April 1914 reported rumours of gun-running and Ulster Volunteer movements the previous night in and around the Musgrave Channel in Belfast, but no concrete information was to hand. On Monday 27 April, they reported the 'arming of Ulster', with the cargo of the 'mysterious' Norwegian steamer *Fanny* being transferred near the Tuskar Light to a vessel 'bearing the name' *Mountjoy*. The latter 'arrived at Larne Harbour late on Friday night.'
> The *Larne Times and Weekly Telegraph* dated Saturday 02 May 1914 heralded:

AMAZING NIGHT AT LARNE
WHOLESALE GUN-RUNNING
THOUSANDS OF RIFLES LANDED
THREE-AND-A-HALF MILLION CARTRIDGES
MOTORS FROM FAR AND NEAR
ASTOUNDING ACHIEVEMENT

In the body of the extensive reports, the role of the RIC in all this was mentioned:

At Drumalis the men were told off into companies, each had their duties allotted to them, and all left Drumalis by different routes, a matter which went a long way towards increasing the embarassment of the police, who were carefully noting all movements ...

The movements of the Volunteers ... completely baffled the police, who were without a clue to the meaning of the hurried and strong mobilisation. So well was the scheme organised and carried through that neither the police nor yet the Customs officers could make their way to the harbour. Every means of access thereto was strongly guarded by determined bands of Volunteers, and when the first attempt to break through the line had failed, the police, evidently realising that the odds against them were too great, contented themselves by acting the role of spectators while cars and lorries laden with "warlike" materials darted past at speed.

All roads leading to Larne were lined with Volunteers for many miles, and this would have rendered any attempt on the part of the police to communicate with other centres entirely useless. In addition, telephone communication was disorganised, and here again it was impossible to communicate with the outside world. Motors having consignments, the destination of which was presumably not very far removed from the town, returned to the harbour again and again, and shortly before four o'clock the last rifle had been removed.

> This hub of Ulster Volunteer activity ironically was where McKenna was posted to within a few months as a punishment (or so he believed) for insisting that he would not misrepresent the number of Ulster Volunteers in the

Carnlough area. His belief that his District Inspector was present at Larne Harbour that night and that the County Inspector's car was used to transport weapons may have been only hearsay, but given the attitude, as he saw it, of the RIC hierarchy in Co. Antrim towards the Ulster Volunteers, it would not have come as a surprise to those of a Nationalist persuasion.

Neither would the supine attitude of the RIC in the town towards Volunteers storing weapons in the Orange Hall just across the road from the police barracks, and their drilling in the market place on 12 July 1914 (see Larne to Kerry section).

In retrospect, the fixing of figures required by his superiors in Carnlough heralded the impossibility of the Loyalist north willingly consenting to be part of a 32 counties Home Rule Parliament controlled by Dublin. The importing of German guns by the Ulster Volunteer Force (UVF) showed the lengths to which the Loyalists would go to prevent Home Rule, and how the 'Orange Card' would be played once again. Only the outbreak of the First World War prevented the situation deteriorating.

First signs of trouble: Larne to Kerry

I HAD EIGHT SMALL CHILDREN, ONE ONLY a fortnight old. It was only on account of them that I did not rebel and refuse to go [to Larne]. Even on the morning I had to leave I had a wire written out to send to the Inspector General, but my poor wife, who is now in heaven I trust, persuaded me not to. There was a section in the code that no man was to be taken out of charge of a station without the sanction of the Inspector General, but in my case these men could give no reason. So it was done contrary to the regulations and because I told the truth.

This was the way these men, who were paid big salaries as government officials, supported the government in power. Their false reports, I have no doubt, did interfere with the passing of the Home Rule Bill[1] and thus were directly responsible for all the bloodshed that has taken place in Ireland since ...

In today's *Irish News* [11 July 1932] I see in extracts from the life of John Redmond where, about the time I write of, he wrote to Asquith[2] suggesting the transfer of County Inspector Morrison of Antrim and Smith of Belfast. What a pity poor old 'Wait and See' didn't act on it. I am satisfied that if there had been police officers in the North then who would do their duty, all the blood that has been shed in Ireland since would have been averted, and that the country would be by now both peaceful and prosperous.

It was about this time (some time prior to this) too that Carson was invited to dine with the Emperor of Germany,[3] and I have no doubt but the threats of this man with his paper army had at least some influence in bringing about the Great War.

I arrived in Larne on the 29 June 1914, thoroughly cut up and downhearted. Up to this time I thought I was in an honourable job, that the police of Ireland, with some rare exceptions, were honestly doing their duty and faithfully carrying out the wishes of whatever government was in power. But from then on, until I left in 1922, my belief in their impartiality kept on dwindling until it disappeared altogether.

On the 11 July 1914, a few days after my arrival in Larne, motor cars from all over the county arrived at the Orange Hall right opposite the police barracks and disgorged their load of arms openly – rifles and bayonets. These were undoubtedly some of those imported illegally, but we police got no orders to do what was our obvious duty – seize them.

Next day, the Volunteers marched openly through the town, 11,000 strong, fully armed and equipped with rifles and bayonets. They drilled openly in the market yard evening after evening of the weeks following until war was declared.[4]

In the meantime the National Volunteers, in imitation of the Ulster Volunteers, had arms imported into Howth [Co. Dublin], but, unlike the way the Ulster lawbreakers were helped by the police authorities, the Dublin men who were imitating them on a much smaller scale were fired upon – three persons were killed and some thirty-eight injured. A typical example of the impartial manner in which the law was enforced in the different parts of the country.

For some years after this there were no more threats of rebellion in Ulster. The Great War was causing anxiety enough and the Home Rule Bill was suspended. Even the rebellion of 1916 in Dublin did not cause any threats in Ulster of a counter-rebellion. Sometime after the rebellion, I was directed to take arms from the Nationalists in Larne. I did so, and was told by the District Inspector that the head of the Ulster Volunteers was to collect the arms from their own men and hand them in.

The arms were similarly taken from the Nationalists all over the North on the same night, but I had good reason afterwards to know that they were not taken from the Ulster Volunteers, as I saw them in use in 1921 on the Twelfth of July in Cookstown. The Orangemen told me they would take them out, and did so, firing volley after volley into Catholic houses in Orritor Street. A truce had been proclaimed at the time and we were not allowed to take out our arms. An Orange sash had allegedly been snatched from a drunken Orangeman. They always alleged that a Catholic had done something to them when they wanted to start terrorism.

The only incident worth recording from the seizure of the arms from the Hibernians in Larne until my arrival in Cookstown was a run to Nenagh, Co. Tipperary, about the month of March 1920, as far as I can remember. A detachment of us were ordered by wire to Nenagh. I had only returned off duty from inspecting weighbridges in Cushendall and had been away for three days when I was told I had to go next day to Nenagh.

It was not my turn for such duty, as I had done several such turns of what was termed public duty, whereas another Sergeant in the station, who was a crouching favourite, had done none. But as it was drawing nearer to my promotion to Head Constable I did not rebel further than to phone Lisburn to know why I was being sent, and was told by one of the clerks that I was specially named by the County Inspector.

Being the senior non-com [non-commissioned officer] I had to take charge of the detachment. Our own District Inspector was with us, but was discreetly inconspicuous and left everything to me. Nobody knew what we were going for or what length of time we were likely to be there, until after travelling all day we arrived in Nenagh some time before 10 pm. We found on arrival there were detachments from several other counties, and the cause of it all was that two brothers named O'Brien were to be tried at the assizes there next day, for the killing of an old man in a raid for the rifle of his son, who was a soldier on furlough during the War.

We got lodgings in the town and found the people very friendly and nice to us. We were told to parade next morning at nine, and as it was a cold March morning we paraded with overcoats on. In the yard we found quite an army of police from Meath and other counties in addition to the local force. Besides the County Inspector who was then a feeble old man, there were a number of District Inspectors including our own and poor Hunt, who was afterwards shot.

Each party was told what their duty was to be and we were informed that we were to be a baton party under DI Hunt, who came over to where we were on parade. Our own DI, with very little consideration for our health and comfort on a cold day in March said, 'Perhaps you would sooner have these men without their overcoats?' to which Hunt replied 'Yes, I would much prefer them without coats', with the result that we were told to take off our coats and 'fall in' with truncheons only.

Having done so, we were marched to the railway station, and on our arrival there we found a company of soldiers in the station yard in the charge of a Sergeant Major. I was put in charge of a gate on the west of the yard with a number of police and told to allow no person to enter or leave by that gate. Another sergeant was put in charge of the other gate leading to the town and each of us had two soldiers with fixed bayonets on either side of our respective gates.

In a short time a covered police motor van arrived. It was the first of its kind I had seen. It was drawn up beside the wicker gate leading from the yard to the platform. I got instructions that as soon as the motor started with the prisoners I was to march my party behind the soldiers. The other Sergeant was directed to march his in front. We were there for about half an hour before the train arrived and attracted no doubt by such a display of force, a few dozen of women and children collected near us, but showed no hostility to us in any way.

When the train arrived, the two prisoners, handcuffed together, were rushed into the back of the van. The door was closed on them and their escort and we all started for the courthouse at a funeral pace. In fact it was very like a funeral – a party of police in front, the all black motor van with a line of soldiers on either side of it and another party of police and soldiers in the rear. We proceeded at this rate through Nenagh, and when we got to within about 100 yards of the courthouse, we were ordered to form a line across the street and put the people back.

It was a Fair Day in the town and a number of country people, attracted no doubt by such a display, were following us purely out of curiosity. The people stopped when we told them and were in no way hostile or threatening, but we were then ordered to put them back. They went back without any of us having to use force; except [for] the District Inspector who used a big walking stick in what I thought was both a cruel and unnecessary manner.

We were kept standing in the street all day in a cold March wind until about 4 o'clock, when the prisoners, having refused to recognise the court, were put back and I was ordered to get my party ready to escort them to Dublin. As soon as we were ready, we went to the station and awaited the arrival of the prisoners, who came back in the same processional order as in the morning.

They came onto the platform some time before the train arrived, and as in the morning some of the people (mostly children) came to the station. There was a bridge across the line on the north side of the station where a road crossed the railway, and while we were waiting I noticed the people on the platform looking towards this bridge and smiling.

I looked also and saw DI Hunt having both a baton charge of police and soldiers charging with bayonets, while a few dozen children were running in front of them. It was the only charge I ever witnessed during 31 years in the police and I have no hesitation in saying that there was not the slightest necessity for it. In a few minutes the train arrived and we took the two prisoners to Dublin, where at Kingsbridge we handed them over to the Dublin Metropolitan Police who were waiting at the station for them.

It was not very long after that I heard that DI Hunt (R.I.P.) was shot in Thurles.[5] I was sorry when I saw his death in the paper, but I was not surprised. I cannot be sure now as to what year it was we were in Nenagh. I know it was the month of March and I know too that there had been no police shot up to this time, except at the rebellion in 1916.

I remember saying at the time that by the unnecessary display of force and aggressive demeanour of poor Hunt, the authorities were asking for trouble. I am sorry to say that they got it and alas (!) some (I should say many) poor innocent policemen lost their lives. I must say here, lest it should be thought that I am condoning any of these shootings, that I utterly detest the killing of any human being.

I could never understand why poor innocent policemen, many of whom were married and struggling hard to keep their families from starving on a miserable income, were shot down by brother Irishmen. Most of them were, I am sure, like myself, entirely ignorant of the history of their country and knew nothing whatever about politics when they joined the police. In order to prove this, I will here relate an incident that took place while I was a recruit in the Depot.

We were all told to assemble on the parade ground, as some great man was coming to say goodbye to us before he left Ireland. We were instructed to put our helmets on the point of our fixed bayonets and cheer as loudly as we could as soon as he finished speaking. He came, and after inspecting us, made a speech telling us we were the finest in the world, etc., and when he had finished I, along with the others, put my helmet on the point of my bayonet and cheered with all my 'might'.

I did not know the man or who he was. I may have heard he was the Chief Secretary[6], but that conveyed nothing to me, as I did not know what the 'Chief Secretary' meant. But years after, when I did begin to know something about how Ireland was governed, I learned that the man I had cheered so lustily was the famous A.J. Balfour.

The system of education, as stated by Miss MacSwiney in her evidence at the Commission, was so arranged that no child got learning anything of the history of their country, and I am certain that 99 per cent of RIC [men] were like myself at the time. They joined entirely ignorant of the history of their country, and neither they nor their parents thought that in becoming a policeman they were doing anything unpatriotic or dishonourable. As years went by, many of them may have learned some history and found that the tendency of the higher authorities was anti-Irish, but by that time they had spent the best years of their lives in the calling of their choice and had been qualifying for a pension.

Many of them were married and struggling to live on a miserable wage, so that it was entirely unreasonable to expect them to throw away their only means of living and leave their wives and children starving. But even if any shooting had to be done, why shoot the poor ignorant, innocent constable who had no opportunity or wish in any way to influence the government in power. It was like a man who wanted to remove a tree, the roots of which were injuring his ground, starting to cut off tiny branches of the top instead of uprooting it.

Anyhow, as I have stated, I detest the shooting or killing of any human being, and besides I believe had Ireland remained true to Mr John Redmond and his party, he would have got the Home Rule Bill eventually put in force over a united Ireland – which would be much better off today had there never been a shot fired or a drop of blood shed.

At present there is nothing but chaos in the so-called Free State, while in the partitioned Six Counties the Catholics haven't the life of a dog under an Orange Government. The Catholics had some degree of liberty while they were governed from London, and if they were in any way ill-treated the Irish Party would expose their ill-treatment in the British House of Commons. Now they can only grin and bear their brutal treatment without any redress – as witness the attack on the pilgrims going to the Congress.

Personally, I must say before I finish this part of my explanation of my own feelings about the shooting of the police, that as far as I was concerned, the Sinn Féiners did nothing nor said anything to me either in Tipperary, Kerry or Kildare. I had no truck or dealing with Sinn Féin any more than I had with the Ulster Volunteers, and during my time in Kerry in 1920 and in Kildare in 1921–22, I went to Mass daily, unarmed and in uniform, and no person ever molested me.

As to the Black and Tans, I found them perfect gentlemen in comparison with the Ulster Specials. No doubt the Tans did some desperate things, but a lot depended on the man in charge of them. I know that I found them more easily controlled than the Specials, and if I had to live that part of my life over again, I would certainly prefer to live with the Tans. That is the irony of the way things have turned. [W.T.] Cosgrave, MacNeill & Co.[7] talk of the freedom of Ireland because they got rid of the Tans in a few counties, never thinking of the plight of the downtrodden Catholics in the North who they have left to the mercy of much greater ruffians.

In 1920 I was promoted to Head Constable and transferred from

Larne to Kenmare, Co. Kerry.[8] It was my turn for promotion, so there was no special favour conferred on me – in fact I was much senior to some who were advanced on the same day. While most of them were kept in what were considered safe stations in the North, I was sent to what was considered the most dangerous county in Ireland. I went through the town of Kenmare where I was a complete stranger, unarmed and in uniform, every morning to the church for Mass. No person ever molested me. But my poor wife and nine children were very anxious about me and wanted me to get back to the North. It was to satisfy them that I applied for a transfer to Cookstown [Co. Tyrone], and was not a little surprised as well as pleased when in a few weeks I got my request.

Notes

1. The Home Rule Bill was introduced in the House of Commons on 11 April 1912. In March, a Home Rule rally in Dublin was matched by an anti-Home Rule rally at Balmoral in Belfast, both attended by around 100,000 people. The Unionist Clubs featured prominently at Balmoral, suggesting a broader based support for the campaign than just the Orange Order. By June 1912, a motion in the Commons proposed excluding the four Counties of Down, Antrim, Derry and Armagh, but was defeated by 69 votes. At the end of June 1912, a clash between Hibernians returning to Castledawson from a parade in Maghera and a Presbyterian Sunday School outing prompted attacks on Catholics in the Belfast Shipyards. This led to around 2,000 Catholics leaving their employment.

In March 1914 John Redmond, leader of the Irish Party in the House of Commons, pledged his support for a scheme whereby separate northern counties could opt out of the proposed Home Rule State for up to three years. This was to be the Government's 'last word' on the matter, and the Irish Party only agreed to the scheme on the understanding that any exclusion would be temporary.

Things changed as the First World War got under way, and Redmond's assumption that his support for the war effort would stand Irish Nationalism in good stead with the Government was to prove mistaken. His condemnation of the 1916 Easter Rising as 'a German plot' was supported by the *Irish News* at the time. For moderate Nationalists, of whom John McKenna was one, it was unthinkable that Ireland could establish total independence from Britain.

Lloyd George (the Munitions Minister during the War), given the task of liaising with Irish politicians, anticipated future juggling acts where policy on Northern Ireland was concerned. He gave Carson a firm assurance that six counties (the present area of Northern Ireland) would be excluded permanently from Home Rule, while at the same time briefing Redmond's party that exclusion would be temporary. By May of 1916 Redmond had agreed to the exclusion of the six counties from Home Rule for the duration of the War, something which did not impress northern Nationalists in Fermanagh and Tyrone. As these two counties had Catholic majorities, their preferred option would have been to opt out, and they would surely have voted accordingly in a county by county referendum.

At an Irish Party conference in Belfast on 23 June 1916, only the powerful oratory and charisma of the northern Nationalist leader, Joe Devlin, prevented a schism in Irish Party ranks. The wide margin in support of Redmond's policy (475 to 265) was belied by the fact that Tyrone and Fermanagh delegates recorded clear majorities against the policy. Antrim and Down, Joe Devlin's natural support base, showed large majorities in favour, with Co. Derry evenly divided, and Derry City against.

2. Asquith does come across as dithering in the events of the time. In July 1913 he gave an assurance that 'The soldiers of the King will not be employed against peaceful Ulster Protestant opposition to Home Rule.' No mention was made as to how he planned to respond to violent Ulster opposition, or at least the threat of such. No such assurance was given in respect of those Irishmen under arms in support of Home Rule, as the British Government did use the 'soldiers of the King' to combat the National Volunteers' activities when three people were killed in Dublin in the aftermath of the Howth gun-running in July 1914.

3. Carson did indeed meet the Kaiser, according to Geoffrey Lewis, *Carson, the Man Who Divided Ireland* (London, 2005), p 121:

> In Aug 1913 Carson was at Homburg as usual when a curious incident occurred. He sat next to the Kaiser at a lunch party. Carson found that he took 'an extraordinary interest' in everything and 'loves a joke'. He was much fascinated by the Emperor's personality, he told Lady Londonderry. The Kaiser remarked that he would have liked to go to Ireland but that his grandmother, Queen Victoria would not let him.

The note sources the story to a letter in the Londonderry Papers (PRONI D654) dated 26 August 1913, suggesting that the meeting took place in the summer of 1913. It seems that Carson was in the habit of frequenting a German spa at Homburg.

4. Carson's belligerence over the period is indisputable. At an UVF rally in September 1913 in Banbridge, he expressed the hope that he would 'see every man with a rifle on his shoulder' the next time he came to inspect them. At another rally, he acknowledged drilling to be illegal, but exhorted his supporters not to be afraid of this, as illegalities 'are not crimes when they are taken to assert what is the elementary right of every citizen – the protection of his freedom.'

5. District Inspector Hunt was killed by the IRA in June 1919 whilst on duty in Thurles in the aftermath of a race meeting taking place in the area at the time. This was only a matter of months after the opening shots in the Irish War of Independence were fired with the killing of two RIC men at Soloheadbeg in Co. Tipperary. McKenna most likely went to Nenagh in March 1918, given his certainty that no policemen had been killed up to the time of which he writes. Also, the trial concerned the attempted theft of a rifle belonging to a soldier home on furlough, which suggests the Great War was still ongoing.

6. Arthur James Balfour was the Chief Secretary for Ireland from 1887 to 1891, the latter year being the year McKenna joined the RIC. He (Balfour) would later become Prime Minister between 1902 and 1905 under the Conservative Party.

7. Eoin MacNeill (1867–1945), was born in Glenarm, Co. Antrim. An historian, he was also a founder of the Gaelic League and the Irish Volunteers. W.T. Cosgrave was the Speaker in Dáil Éireann between 1919–21; he was also Minister of Education in the Free State government 1922–5.

8. McKenna's stay in Kerry was a brief one of about seven weeks. It is unlikely he would have found an extended posting there much more congenial than his time in Cookstown, given the assassination campaign against RIC men which was well under way at the time – September 1920. Remarkably, considering the short period he was actually in Kenmare, there exists a reference to him in the reminiscences of another RIC man, William Dunne.

The following passage relates to an incident in Kerry when William Dunne was evacuated from the barracks between Kenmare and Killarney to make way for the Army. Dunne and his colleagues were considered to be in too dangerous a location, being isolated and vulnerable to attack in the small barracks. They went by boat (the *Anthony Essex*) to Ennisfeirt, where the locals showed hostility towards them. From there they made their way to Tralee where the police didn't know what to do with them. They were sent back by train to Kenmare in plain clothes (five or six of them), carrying their possessions in 'tea chests covered in canvas'.

The reminiscence was taken by John Brewer in the 1980's, when Dunne was an old man in his nineties, but a young man when he joined the RIC in 1917.

> We came to the junction called Kettrick junction, where the military was ambushed one time. There was a man standing very uneasy, very interested in us, you see. Now we were in plain clothes and we had tea chests covered in canvas. So we went to question him to see who he was and he was the Head Constable going to our station on transfer, on promotion. He was coming from Larne, a very decent man. He thought we were after raiding some Barrack, that we were some sort of IRA men.

Kettrick junction may have been a railway halt where the RIC men got off. Presumably McKenna had literally just got off the train from Larne (no doubt after many changes and breaks in the journey), as he must have been in civilian clothes himself, given how the RIC men did not know straight away he was a policeman. McKenna's family stayed in Larne, where they had by this time settled, with the younger children's schooling liable to disruption had another move been undertaken.

McKenna's favourable view of Kerry may have been coloured by the briefness of the time he was there, and he may have presented a more agreeable face to actual or potential IRA supporters than perhaps DI Hunt did. The Loyalist north was another world from that of Republican Kerry, but the dissent in the two different ends of the country would ultimately squeeze out from the RIC constitutional nationalists such as McKenna who did not belong to either world.

Cookstown: into a flaming cauldron

IT WAS THE FIRST TIME THAT I USED OUTSIDE influence to obtain a favour, and before many months went by no man could have regretted more than I did having done so. Of course, it was all my own fault. Had I been able to enjoy looking on while unfortunate Catholics were being maltreated and terrorised; when outrages were committed by Specials and other followers of Carson & Co. and Catholics blamed for them, or laugh when reprisals were carried out on Catholics by those same Specials for the crimes committed by themselves, I would have had the best of a time, but I could not do so, and when I tried to stop such horrible things being done I was only a 'Bloody Papish.'

That was the reply given by the men, who had [taken] out Carson's guns on the Twelfth of July 1921, to a Black and Tan named Wilson when asked why they would think of shooting a man who had served 30 years in the RIC, as I had. Wilson was an Englishman and, I must say, a very manly, decent little man. He was a Protestant of some denomination, but he could not understand the Orangemen ... He was in the crowd that night along with some other Protestant policemen of my own station. I had a Special Constable named Swindall with me. Poor Swindall, he was one of the few decent, innocent Specials I had. He and I were up Orritor Street [the main nationalist street in Cookstown] looking for a man who was supposed to have taken an Orangeman's sash.

The heroes with the guns were at the corner of Orritor and Oldtown Streets. I was the only Catholic out of doors in Cookstown at the time, and Swindall, knowing the danger I was in, begged me to return to the barracks, but I said no. The poor lad then said, 'Just think, Head, what might happen to your wife and children if anything should happen to you.'

I said, 'Why should anything happen to me?' But I could see that while he knew well that I was in danger, he was afraid to give the show away by telling me plainly what he thought. I remained on the street until the fury of the Orangemen had spent itself. I could do nothing. The truce [arranged between the British government and Sinn Féin in July 1921] was on and I couldn't take out arms, and I could not tackle single-handed hundreds of mad Orangemen armed with rifles and firing bullets.[1]

It was next day, when I had Wilson out with me, that I said to him I was sure he heard the Orangemen saying some nice things about me the previous night. He said, 'If only you knew just what they were saying about you.'

I said, 'I suppose they were talking about making holes through me.' To which he replied, 'It was only a question of getting Swindall away from you.' I then said, 'And what did you say to them?'

'I said, why should you do that to a man who served 30 years in the RIC? They replied, "he bedamned. He's only a Bloody Papish".'

These were the men the British Government were trying to make the world believe were assisting me in doing police duty. Of course I knew what Wilson told me was true, but I pretended to Swindall, while the guns were barking out bullets, that I was in no danger. I knew well enough that I was, but that if they were going to fire on us they might kill him too. Had I gone down that night, the most horrible part of it would be that they would have said it was Sinn Féiners did it, and would have had reprisals on some Catholics for the killing of me.

I saw some months ago where Sir Dawson Bates [Northern Ireland Minister of Home Affairs, 1921–43], answering a question about the Ballinderry shooting outrage[2] on St. Patrick's Day last, stated as a reason why the charges made against the police for not doing their duty were not true – was the fact that the Head Constable was a Catholic! On the contrary, that fact would only cause the Specials and others to commit outrages.

The District Inspector and the men in the lower ranks, in collusion with the 'B' men and their sympathisers, would leave the

Catholic Head Constable as useless as a child. He would only be useful in the sense that Sir Dawson Bates used him as a cloak to show how impartial they were.

In this connection I may here give an incident which will prove what I stated above. After we had the Specials enrolled, they were not satisfied until they had work to do. There was nothing for them to do, but I was ordered to employ them on patrols at night. I had to send one RIC man with about 20 'B' men, fully armed with rifle, bayonet and 100 rounds of ammunition, on patrol each night. I was to give the RIC man instructions as to the direction he was to take and the roads to be followed. Had I been allowed any discretion in the matter, I would not have allowed them out at all, but although I was supposed to be responsible for the peace of the district, I had no option.

On one particular night I sent an RIC man named Henderson with the 'B' men, and gave him instructions to go in a certain direction. On the following morning a poor old man and his wife called at the barrack to complain that their house was raided by police, their sons taken out and beaten, put on their knees and told they would be shot, etc. This man lived in a locality miles away from that to which I had sent the patrol. There was a book called the 'patrol book' in which particulars of each patrol had to be entered by the man in charge of the patrol.

I then examined this book and found that Henderson had entered that the patrol had entered this poor man's house, and had not gone in the direction I had sent him. When I questioned him with a view to reporting him for disobedience of orders, he told me that the District Inspector met them and told them to raid this house.

The whole trouble at this time was that Catholics in and around Cookstown were keeping too quiet, and there was no real work for the Specials to do. It was just about the time when the 'B' men got their waterproof coats and caps (they had their arms and ammunition prior to this), that one night, about 10 pm, just after I returned to the barracks, a knock was heard at the door.

On answering it, I found that it was the wife of the District Inspector [George Hall, DI for Cookstown], who lived next door looking for me, saying that her husband had sent her to tell me their servant's hair had been cut off by two men. I took a man with me and went into the DI's house along with his wife. In the kitchen I found the DI and the 'B' Head Constable, Sidney McClelland, along with the alleged injured girl, Minnie Reilly. She told me that, only a few minutes previously, she had been pulled into a gateway and had her hair cut off. I asked for a description [of her assailants], but she couldn't say what they were like, only that one of them was long, or tall, and the other short.

It seemed strange that my own District Inspector, who was my superior and drawing much more money from the state than I was, should be sitting comfortably in the kitchen with the 'B' Head Constable after hearing of this outrage on his own servant. Both he and the 'B' man knew the people, whereas I was only a stranger, and yet it was to me he had sent his wife. So after I had questioned the girl for some minutes, I said that I supposed we could do nothing and went to return to the barracks. As I was going out, his wife said to me, what about looking for the hair, Head? I said I thought it would be useless, but she persisted that we should look for it. We did so, and one of the men found it on the pavement within about 20 yards of the DI's house. When I returned to the barracks that night I was in an awful state of mind.³

I went to bed but I could not sleep. It was quite evident who the long and short men were who cut Minnie Reilly's hair off, and that she knew too, but what could I do? I could prove nothing, but if I didn't sleep any that night, I put in a much more miserable time the following night.

Next day the 'outrage' was reported and the District Inspector got in communication with the 'A' Platoons of Specials of Dungannon and Magherafelt. They were all to arrive in Cookstown at about 10 pm. I asked him what they were going to do when they came and he said, 'Oh, Head, we will have to make a search.'

I said, 'What are we to search for? Is it the scissors, and if so, how are we to know the one that was used?' He then said, 'Oh you know Head, we must do something to keep the 'B' men quiet.' That answer of his told everything: why the hair was cut off, etc.

Anyhow, the Specials arrived at about 10 pm. It was winter [it was actually April] time and the night was dark. They came in Crossley cars and in such numbers that there wasn't standing room for them in the barrack. The District Inspector and the 'B' Head detailed us off into parties to go through the town of Cookstown and search respectable Catholic houses. None of us knew what we were looking for. Of course I had been told that the outrages we were committing were being done to keep the 'B' men quiet.

After we had committed these outrages and found nothing, we returned to the barracks and the Specials went back home, but for me there was no sleep. I went to bed, but instead of sleeping, I am not ashamed to say it, that man though I was, I cried like a child until morning. I saw how helpless I was in being compelled to assist in committing such outrages on decent, innocent people. It was horrible to think that after having spent 30 years in what I thought was an honourable job, to find it so rotten, and having actually to take part in such foul deeds. Of course it was only consideration of my family that made me stick it, and I daresay they will never realise what a sacrifice I was making in doing so.

I had afterwards to give evidence of finding the hair when the poor dupe Minnie Reilly claimed compensation, but I was not asked for my opinion. Had I been and answered truthfully, my answers would, I am sure, have staggered the judge. It was not even opposed. The solicitor who acted for the ratepayers was of the same way of thinking as the manufacturers of the 'outrage' and Minnie was awarded £10 compensation. The 'bobbed hair' was just then beginning to become fashionable and any hairdresser would have charged her a shilling for doing what was done to her hair. In addition to getting something for the 'B' men to do and to justify their existence, there was another reason why outrages were necessary.

The 'B' Head Constable had previously told me when I was enquiring into another alleged malicious injury claim that the Catholics of Cookstown were the largest ratepayers. So that in addition to being terrorised by the 'B' men, they would have to pay most of the compensation awarded for these bogus outrages.[4]

Before beginning to describe a number of these bogus outrages in which I was more or less involved, I will set down here particulars of the only genuine Sinn Féin outrage which occurred when I was in the district.

A rural postman was returning from a place called Dunamore one evening and was held up by two armed and masked men. His postbag and letters were taken. On the same evening, a Catholic resident came to me and gave me information which caused us to suspect a young man named John McDermott, a student who was home on holidays from Newbridge College [Co. Kildare]. He lived with his father near Dunamore. The following day, the District Inspector got into communication with the 'B' platoon commander at Magherafelt and arranged that he would send a platoon early next morning to assist in the searching for McDermott.

After he had all arranged, he said to me several times, 'I wonder, Head, should I go with you,' from which I inferred that, whether he faced the danger zone or not, there was no doubt that I would have to. However, I only replied that he could do whatever he wished. Eventually he decided that he would come with us, and he would wear a Constable's coat so that he would not be known. And on the next morning, he dressed in a Constable's waterproof coat and accompanied us to Dunamore in the Crossley cars.

We reached McDermott's house and found only the old man there. The District Inspector and the platoon commander kept discreetly outside, and as we were about to leave, young McDermott walked into the kitchen. I found him with his hands up very high and two bayonets against his chest. There were shouts of 'put them up higher,' but on seeing that he could not put them any higher up, I released him from his uncomfortable position and put two men in charge of him.

I went and informed the District Inspector that McDermott was inside, to which he replied, 'Oh Head, you had better arrest him – it doesn't suit me going to courtsmartial, so you had better arrest him.' I then went and arrested John McDermott and having handcuffed and cautioned him, put him in one of the cars, and proceeded to the house of the man who was with him at the 'hold-up'.

On going into this house, the District Inspector sat down at the kitchen table and took out his loaded revolver and left it on the table. He was so nervous and excited that he got up and went outside, leaving the revolver on the table. I picked it up and put it in my pocket, and on returning to the cars I handed it to him asking if it were his. He then realised what he had done and said, 'Oh good God, Head, isn't that an awful thing I did. Wasn't it well you got it?'

Had any of the men in the house been so inclined, they could have shot six of us with our own gun and ammunition. Yet shortly afterwards this hero got the MBE after his name for distinguished service.

We brought the prisoner to the barracks and put him in the cell. On the same evening, or next day, I arrested a young fellow named Hagan who drove the car in which McDermott and the other man were driven to the 'hold-up'. As the weather was cold, I made the orderly let them sit at the dayroom fire, and by this simple act of human charity I made myself very unpopular with the Specials, and others, both in the barracks and outside. They were sent to Derry for trial by court martial, and McDermott got five years, the others getting shorter sentences of six months or thereabouts.

It was while I was absent in Derry that the first of the doubtful attacks occurred. On opening the morning's paper in Derry, I found it reported that the District Inspector's house in Cookstown was fired into. After I returned from Derry, I learned there were two alleged attacks. On the second occasion, Sergeant Dunne and a constable were on the ground floor, along with the DI, and on his going upstairs there was a crash of broken glass. The Sergeant and Constable rushed upstairs and found the window broken, but could find no trace of bullets or other missile with which it was broken. The sequel was that a better house next door to the barracks was commandeered for the DI, while the incident provided still another reason for the existence of the Specials.

It was about this time that we opened two new stations, one at Rock and another at a place known as Kildress. We were crowded out with Specials in Cookstown, so two houses were commandeered, and a sergeant and a number of constables and Specials put into each of them. Everything was quiet in both places before the stations were opened, but before the police were long there, there was a big change. The 'B' Specials, with one RIC man in charge (usually a Black and Tan), began patrolling at night.

One Sunday, some weeks after the opening of the Kildress station, as I was about to start for a home run to Larne, the District Inspector sent for me and told me that I should go with him to Kildress. A man had been shot. I went with him, and on our arrival, I had a conversation with the sergeant, a Catholic named Lynham. He told me that, the previous night, he sent an English Black and Tan along with the 'B' men on patrol. On his return, about 1 am, he reported that they had entered the house of a Catholic, and brought out the son. When he was outside he [the suspect] went to run away. The 'B' men fired on him, wounding him in the lung. While the sergeant and I were talking, the DI was speaking to the Black and Tan.

After talking to him for some time in the barracks, he took him out, and they both of them walked away from the barracks about 100 yards. While they were out, I asked the sergeant if the Black and Tan would stick to his original statement, and he said he thought he would. I said to him I would be prepared to wager any sum he wanted to name that, when he (the Black and Tan) came in again, he would tell a different story. I had scarcely said these words when the District Inspector and the Tan came in.

The District Inspector said, 'It's all right, the man was hiding behind a fence. They thought he was going to ambush them and when he jumped out and ran away, they called on him to halt. When he did not, they fired and wounded him.' He then took me to the house where this poor unfortunate victim was lying in bed with a bullet wound through his lung.

His mother and sister told us how they (the Specials) came and took him out, and in a short time they heard shots. They went out and found him lying some yards away wounded. My state of mind can be imagined while I listened to my superior telling these poor people how he would seek out the culprit, knowing as I did how he had already got the Black and Tan who was in charge of the patrol to make a false statement, with a view to justifying the shooting. I did not think the poor fellow who was wounded would live, but luckily he did. I was glad to learn, after I had left the District, that he was allowed a sum of money by the County Court Judge.

The Opening of Rock Station[5]

Some time after the above incident, negotiations were going on about opening a station at Rock. There had been a police station there previously but in compliance with an order from Dublin Castle, it was vacated before I went to Cookstown, and the house was burnt after the police left. A man named Thomas Beck had two public houses in the village, in one of which he lived. The other was vacant and was in my opinion more suitable for a barrack than Beck's house which had been his home for generations. He even offered us the vacant house, and as I knew him to be a decent man, knowing also the awful upset it would be to him and his family to be put out of the house they were in, I tried to get the District Inspector to take the vacant house. He promised to do so, but on the morning we were to take the house he (the DI) went off with the military officer who was to do the commandeering, leaving me to take charge of the transport, conveying the barrack furniture, etc. On my arrival in Rock I found the Specials carrying out furniture etc., from the house occupied by Mr. Beck and his family. His wife and daughter were crying, and although I had never seen them until that day, I felt sorry for them. I thought it a heartless and vindictive use of authority, as the other house, which was empty, was better suited for a barrack.

But Beck was a Catholic, and here was an opportunity for crushing the spirit out of him. At any rate we evicted him and put in the police and their furniture, barricaded the house and left a Sergeant Gallagher and a party of Specials in it.

Notes

1. In the *Irish News* dated Thursday 14 July 1921, the Twelfth night in Cookstown was reported under the following headlines:

COOKSTOWN ORGY
Savage Attack of Catholic Inhabitants

HEAVY RIFLE FIRE
– Police Powerless Against Fury of Mob –
MANY HOUSES RUINED.

Wild scenes of disorder, lasting for several hours, occurred in Cookstown on Tuesday night, when a fierce attack was launched on Orritor Street, the principal Catholic quarter, by an Orange mob. The trouble is said to have arisen over the snatching of a sash from an Orangeman by some irresponsible individuals, and despite the fact that the police and several citizens used their best endeavour to have the missing regalia restored under peaceful conditions, this did not satisfy the members of the mob, who proceeded to wreak their vengeance on unoffending citizens. In its character and violence, the outbreak was such as has never before been equalled in the town, even during the most serious riots of the past.

A large crowd, numbering not less than 500, invaded the street about 10.30 pm., demanding the restoration of the sash, but the police kept them in control for well over an hour, when the mob, well reinforced by this time, commenced to fire at the windows of the houses, volley after volley being poured into them, causing much damage to eleven houses.

INVALID IN PERIL

One little thatched house, inhabited by an invalid named Charles Gillen, was wantonly set on fire, the old man having to be rescued through a back window. Attempts to fire another house failed. The Fire Brigade, on reaching the scene, were threatened, but they succeeded in putting on a line of hose and extinguishing the fire and saving the house. The greatest alarm prevailed in the town, the unfortunate inhabitants of Orritor Street being panic-stricken, owing to the terrorism of these hooligans, who, fully armed with service rifles, kept firing into the houses for over four hours.

THE POLICE WERE ABSOLUTELY POWERLESS.

When at last matters settled down, hundreds of empty cartridges and rifle clips were found on the street, which, with its broken windows and smoking roof, had every appearance of having withstood a fierce siege. The Catholics bravely defended their homes as best they could, but against overwhelming forces heavily armed they were powerless.

SEVEN FAMILIES HOMELESS.

As a result of the terrible orgy Orritor Street has been almost completely wrecked, and seven families have been rendered homeless, and were yesterday engaged in removing the little furniture that remained after the wreckage. The mob which participated in the attack got entirely out of control of its leaders, who in some instances tried to intervene, but without avail. Even the town clerk (Mr W.J. Fleming), when conveying the fire hose to a burning house, was threatened with dire penalties if he gave assistance, but he pluckily went on, and with the aid of others partially extinguished the fire which the attackers had started in the thatch of the house of Charles Gillen who is almost eighty years of age and bedridden. The roof was completely burned.

THE HAVOC WROUGHT.

The house occupied by Mr Sam Humphrey was practically riddled with bullets. One of the bullets smashed a valuable lamp, which nearly set the house on fire through burning the curtain on the window. Mr Humphrey himself had a very narrow escape from death, a bullet striking the window beside him. He and his wife and family have left their dwelling in fear of their lives, as also have Mrs Doyle, a next door neighbour, and James Cosgrove, a married man with a wife and small family ... likewise James Smith, Mrs McDonald (an aged widow) William Darragh, and Mr W.J. Windsor, merchant tailor.

The house occupied by Mr Henry McAnespie, furniture and antiques dealer was also visited, and after two attempts at setting it on fire by sprinkling petrol on the door, the latter was broken in. The houses occupied by McAnespie, his wife, his daughter and their children were also wrecked. The raiders proceeded to the front room and smashed some very valuable furniture, including a valuable tantalus of Waterford glass, and in all the other cases the windows were smashed. The mob also wrecked the shop adjoining. The house of Joseph Hagan, where his sick uncle lies almost on the verge of death, was also attacked, the stones and bullets crossing the old man's bed. The house of Mr J. Windsor was completely wrecked, the fine shop windows being smashed to atoms.

At the house occupied by Mr John McGahan an attempt was made to start a fire, and the frontage bears the traces of the petrol used. Young McGahan, in attempting to get out, had petrol thrown on his face, which is badly scorched. The side window of the Belfast House, owned by Mrs Small, one of the most popular spirit merchants in the town, was also broken.

Other residents of the street who suffered injury to their houses are – Miss McKeown, William Turton, James Smith, Mrs McDonald, Miss McCullough, Mrs Mary Jane McCann, Miss Annie Donnelly, Hugh Canavan, Mrs Lappin and James Kearney; also an unoccupied house belonging to James Mooney. In practically all these cases the windows have been broken either by stones or bullets, and on their front walls they all bear bullet marks.

The spent cartridges prove that there is not the slightest doubt that

IT WAS U.V.F. AMMUNITION THAT WAS SO FREELY USED.

During the course of yesterday evening Mr. George Hall, DI,

and H.C. McKenna made a tour of inspection of the wrecked street, ascertaining particulars of the occurrence. At present there is no adequate protection for the Catholics of Cookstown should another outburst of the same nature on defenceless women and children take place.

A report on criminal damages claims in the *Tyrone Courier* of 25 August 1921 verified some of the names in the *Irish News* reports on the damage caused to property on the Twelfth night. Under the heading 'ORRITOR STREET', residents of that street who put in claims included Margaret McCullagh, Daniel Mooney, John McGahan, Robert Darragh, Sarah McDonald, James Cosgrove, William Turton, Samuel Humphrey, Henry Boyd Eastwood, Thomas Joseph Eastwood, James Eastwood and Charles Gillen.

The two largest claims were by Henry McAnespy for '£168 for antique and modern furniture, paintings, pictures, engravings, china glass, curios, ornaments, lustre ware, auto knitting machine, etc.,' and William Francis Eastwood for £260 'for a dwelling house in Orritor Street burned down and destroyed, and the doors and door frames and window frames and sashes of four other dwelling houses, broken damaged and injured.'

The *Newsletter* of Wednesday 13 July 1921 covered the same events under the following headlines:

COOKSTOWN DISTURBANCES
Orange Sash Stolen: Revolver Firing Last Night.

There was some revolver firing in Cookstown last night, or early this morning, following an assault on an Orangeman who was on his way home after the July demonstration. It appears that this man's sash was stolen by his assailants and at about 10 pm an angry crowd attempted to invade the district in which it was believed the sash was to be found. A party of police, under Head Constable McKenna, succeeded, however, in keeping the crowd away; but at about midnight revolver firing was heard, many rounds being fired. By 2 am the disturbance had subsided and no more casualties had been reported up to then.

This was the *Newsletter*'s report in its entirety, and its brevity contrasted sharply with the extensive one in the *Irish News*, even allowing for the fact that the Nationalist paper had another day in which to collate their information.

However, under the same heading as above, i.e. 'Cookstown Disturbances', another incident in the town was given almost equal space to the Twelfth night report:

MORE REBEL PROVOCATION
The 'Truce' Broken by Would-be Incendiaries.

At 12.30 yesterday morning, 12 hours after the 'truce' commenced, an attempt was made to fire the premises of Mr James McGurkin, a Cookstown Unionist, whose motor cars have been frequently used by the police.

Mr McGurkin was aroused by the barking of a dog, and dispatched one of his sons to the yard of his Oldtown Street premises, where it was found that a bag, saturated with paraffin, had been lighted and pushed under the door of a shed, evidently by persons who could be heard making off. Fortunately the flames were extinguished before much damage had been done.

> The *Newsletter* left their readers to draw their own conclusions, with the implication being that the mayhem on the Twelfth night was as a result of IRA provocation. The paper also steered clear of any suggestion that rifles were used on the Twelfth night, mentioning only revolver fire.
> The *Newsletter* revisited the Cookstown story in the following day's edition (Thursday 14 July 1921) under the headlines:

THE COOKSTOWN DISTURBANCE
A Priest's Admission

Further particulars of Tuesday night's disturbances at Cookstown show that as an Orangeman, Albert Creighton, and another man were cycling home, they were attacked by a crowd of hooligans, at least two of whom were armed. The sash Creighton was wearing was torn from him and carried away.

When Creighton reported the matter a number of his friends assembled for the purpose, evidently, of searching for the missing sash. Matters assumed a threatening aspect, and the police appealed to Rev. J. McLaughlin, a priest, for assistance, but he confessed he had no control over the ringleaders.

> About midnight shots were fired from Orritor Street at the Orangemen, some of whom then made an assault on the Roman Catholic quarter and two homes were set on fire. The wiser element prevailed, and the fires were extinguished before much harm was done.
>
> The missing sash was found yesterday morning near the police barracks and subsequently returned to the owner.

This article implied that not only were Republicans firing guns on the Twelfth night, but also that they brought the trouble in the town on the heads of their own community. More puzzling is why the Republicans saw fit to return the presumably intact sash to (near enough) the police station.

The *Irish Times* of 14 July suggested that police in Cookstown arrested a Catholic man named Devlin as being suspected of stealing the sash, 'but on the way to the barracks they were "rushed" by an Orange crowd, and being unable to protect the prisoner, let him go.' The report also mentioned that the police sought assistance from a Presbyterian clergyman in an effort to quell the disturbances. 'The police were in charge of Head Constable McKenna, in the absence of the District Inspector at the assizes.'

The *Tyrone Courier* of Thursday 14 July 1921 neatly encapsulated the Twelfth disturbances in Cookstown in one short paragraph under its diary column:

> In Cookstown on the Twelfth the taking of a sash from an Orangeman on his way home led to revolver firing. There were happily no casualties. An attempt to fire the garage of Mr Jas. McGurkin, a Cookstown Unionist was discovered and the flames extinguished before much damage had been done.

This was the sum total of the Dungannon-based newspaper's coverage of Cookstown disturbances on the Twelfth, and like the *Newsletter* it devoted almost equal column space to Mr McGurkin's mishap as to the events later that night.

The *Tyrone Constitution* of Friday 15 July mentioned the name of the Catholic arrested on the Twelfth night as Devlin, something which caused great hilarity when Joe Devlin, the Northern Nationalist leader, raised the matter of the disturbances in the House of Commons at Westminster. The report also explicitly stated that during the struggle with the Cookstown Devlin,

> shots were fired from the Sinn Féin quarter – Orritor Street. The police kept the crowd in hand for two hours, but it ulti-

mately got out of control, and rushed Orritor Street. Shots were fired from both sides.

> The *Constitution* reported the Solicitor General's opinion that 'RIC men and not Specials were engaged in quelling the Sinn Féin revolt.' However, they also reported that Mr Harbinson, the Irish Party MP for the area, asked in the Commons

if the RIC arrested a man named Devlin to placate the mob, which subsequently threatened the police, and gave Devlin a most unmerciful beating.

> The *Ulster Herald* of Saturday 16 July offered a different perspective, saying that the theft of the sash

was made the excuse for a savage onslaught on the residences of Catholics in Orritor Street. For over two hours during the night volleys of rifle and revolver fire were directed at the houses ...

> The report concluded by confirming that the lost sash 'was found in the morning on a window near the RIC barracks.'
> McKenna's view of the sash incident coincided with that of the *Herald*, yet he did not mention the RIC under his command arresting a Catholic that night. The *Dungannon Democrat* edition of Wednesday 29 July went even further, reporting Harbinson, the local MP, as asking in the Commons if the Chief Secretary for Ireland was aware that

Special Constables, accompanied by an Orange mob, attacked the Catholic quarter of the town [Cookstown], burning a house, from which an invalid had to be carried.

> This supported McKenna's view that the Specials were not so much helping the regular police as helping the Orange mob and possibly even threatening his life.
> However, the *Democrat* did acknowledge, via Mr Harbinson in the Commons, that 'shots were fired by both sides', and when the

Orange mob went up the street ... sprinkling the doors with petrol ... then, in self-defence, two revolver shots were fired from the Catholic quarter, which had the effect of saving the whole street from being burned down.

> Yet the events of that night were passed over as being of trivial importance in

The 'B' Specials – A history of the Ulster Special Constabulary by Sir Arthur Hezlet (Mourne River Press, Belfast 1997). On page 46, we are told that

> Throughout the province [in 1921] the anniversary of the Battle of the Boyne on 12 July was celebrated without disturbances except a minor one in Cookstown when an Orange sash was stolen by some Sinn Féiners.

No doubt there were hotheads on both sides of the conflict, given the emotions that the Twelfth would have generated in Tyrone in 1921. In the aftermath of the then recent activities of the Specials, including the slaying of Joseph Hayden (see next section), it is surprising that serious injuries were not incurred that night. Yet as far as the *Ulster Herald* (16 July) could ascertain, 'only one man was slightly injured in the attack.'

The extensive *Irish News* report went into perhaps unnecessary detail, reflecting the fears in the nationalist community as to what side of the proposed border Tyrone would end up on. As McKenna mentioned in his memoir, the RIC considered itself bound by the Truce and could not take out their weapons in order to control the mob.

The British presence which he supported as a policeman no longer inspired him with the confidence he may once have felt in Galway during what must have seemed like, even in the 1920's, a different era. His role as the only Catholic policeman out on the Twelfth night must have brought home to him his isolation, both from his own colleagues and his co-religionists.

McKenna was alienated from Republicanism and Loyalism, both of which made Redmond's Nationalism seem outdated and naive in the north's sectarian maelstrom. The siege of Catholics by Loyalists, and of Loyalists by Republicanism in Ireland as a whole, meant that things were no longer as simple as they had once appeared to be.

2. On St. Patrick's Day 1932 two AOH (Hibernians) members were shot and injured at Ballinderry Bridge, Co. Tyrone, whilst part of what would now be termed a feeder parade prior to the main Kilrea demonstration. McKenna's concern at the inaction of the RUC in protecting the marchers or apprehending the assailants reflected his disgust at the similar lack of resolve where the Eucharistic Congress procession in Larne was concerned. As a former policeman, he would have had strong views on how the still relatively new administration in Northern Ireland applied the law.

3. McKenna's view that this was an incident staged by the Specials and his DI in order to provide a pretext for raiding Catholic houses is not borne out by the official record. The incident is mentioned briefly (pp. 84–5) in Robert Lynch's *The Northern IRA and the Early Years of Partition 1920–22* (Irish Academic Press, Dublin, 2006).

> The Catholic community also felt the IRA's wrath as the newly confident movement sought out perceived collaborators and spies. In one such inci-

dent a servant girl of the local RIC District Inspector in Tyrone was dragged from her house and had her hair cut off by a gang of Volunteers.

The same incident is mentioned in Hezlet's *The 'B' Specials – A History of the Ulster Special Constabulary*, '... a servant girl in the house of a District Inspector had her hair cut off as she refused to give information about him to the IRA.' (p. 38, mentioned in the context of events in April 1921.)

The *Tyrone Courier* provided an interesting contrast to McKenna's considering the incident a bogus attack by the Specials. From *Courier Diary* of 16 June 1921:

> Miss Minnie Reilly, whose hair was cut off by a couple of miscreants in Cookstown because she pluckily refused to give information about District Inspector Hall's house, was awarded £10 compensation by the Judge, who complimented her on her courage.

If McKenna's perception of the incident was correct, it illustrated the lengths to which the Northern RIC officer class and their allies in the Specials were prepared to go in their efforts to support the embryonic Northern Ireland state. It was becoming evident that the new state and its supporters would not let the scruples of Catholic Nationalist officers prevent them adopting what the historian Patrick Buckland (*The Factory of Grievances: Devolved Government in Northern Ireland 1921–39*) has termed 'a sectarian security policy' in the early 1920s.

(4) The Criminal Injuries records of the time showed that Minnie Reilly claimed £100 for malicious injuries for the incident which occurred on 27 April 1921 at Loy, Cookstown. She was awarded £10, which was 'to be levied off the County at large'. John McKenna, Head Constable RIC, was recorded as being witness to the event.

(5) McKenna put this heading in the original memoir himself.

Rock and a hard place: The Joseph Hayden killing

IN ABOUT A WEEK OR TEN DAYS AFTER the opening of Rock [RIC barracks], the Sergeant sent in a report one morning (about 7 am) to the District Inspector, stating that the house of a family named Hayden had been raided during the night, and that Joseph Hayden was killed and another brother wounded. The DI and I, accompanied by a party of Specials and some Tans, went out in a Crossley tender. When we arrived, we found the body of Joe Hayden in a bed with a bullet wound in his forehead, and a bayonet wound in his heart.

His brother, who had been wounded, had been removed to his mother's house and I did not see him, as I was directed to remain with the corpse. But I was told that the wounded man had a bayonet wound through his lung, and that he said it was Specials in police uniform who raided the house, killing his brother and wounding him. He was very weak, and in a statement mentioned the name of a neighbouring farmer, who was not a Special, as being amongst them. The DI and Sergeant Gallagher, after visiting the wounded man and getting his statement, went to the neighbouring farmer mentioned by him and took a statement from him.

This statement, which I did not see, contained (as I later discovered) an account of how the 'B' men called at his house the previous night and asked where Haydens' house was. In the meantime, we who were left with the dead body had found a policeman's oil bottle in the bed where the murdered man was laid, and a few yards from the door part of the stock of a service rifle was also found.

When the District Inspector (and the Sergeant) returned to us, we were told about the wounded man having mentioned the neighbouring farmer, and that he had taken a statement from the farmer in which he denied being there at all. I said I thought it a strange proceeding to take a statement from a man who was mentioned as having committed a murder, but he did not tell me that the farmer had told him who the murderers were.

I then told the District Inspector about the finding the bottle and part of the rifle, adding that we should go to Tullyhogue, where the 'B' men kept their arms, and find out who was in the patrol, and which rifle the piece of stock and oil bottle were missing from. He said he would first have to wire to Dublin, asking for a military enquiry instead of an inquest by a coroner's jury. A jury would bring a true verdict, and that was not wanted.

On our return to Cookstown, we visited the house of Colonel Lowis of Tullyhogue, who was the local commander of the 'B' men. He had been sending out patrols without any RIC men with them. As soon as we met the Colonel, I asked him who was on patrol the previous night. Before he could answer me, the DI interrupted me and said, 'Easy now, Head, we cannot be probing this thing too closely. These men are police like ourselves,' thus preventing me from doing what was my and his obvious duty, i.e. tracing the murderers. At the same time, this put the Colonel from answering my question.

What, I ask, could I do? My superior would not allow me to do my duty. He would not allow the coroner to hold an inquest, so we all returned to Cookstown and did nothing. On our return to barracks, the District Inspector reported the occurrence to the competent military authority, etc., giving the name of the farmer as being mentioned by the wounded man. Two young military officers arrived at the house on the morning of the funeral and commenced holding an enquiry as to the cause of death. But as Mr Hoy, a Dungannon solicitor representing the relatives, objected to the proceedings, no evidence was given except that of identification and the body was removed for burial.

Either that day or the next ... an order came from the competent military authority to whom the case had been reported to arrest the farmer mentioned in the wounded man's statement. He was duly arrested and brought to Cookstown. While he was in Cookstown barracks dayroom, Colonel McClintock, County Commander of the Specials, came to the barracks. I was in the DI's office attending to the official correspondence.

The District Inspector, Colonel McClintock and the prisoner came into the office, and I, who had then spent over 30 years faithful service in the RIC, was asked by the DI to leave the office in order that they might have a conversation with this man, who was in custody on a charge of murder. He was, however, as I subsequently found out, well-known by them to be innocent, and was only detained for the purpose of shielding the real murderers. That was the reason I was asked to leave the room, as being a Catholic I was not to be trusted. After they had talked to him for some time he was sent to Derry gaol on a detention order.

A few days later, the DI went on holidays and I was left to act in his absence. The statement made by the wounded man Hayden also mentioned the farmer's brother and a servant man of theirs named (I think) Devlin. Just after the DI left, an order came by a code wire for me to have these two men arrested also and brought to Derry. I had them arrested and sent to Derry on the same day.

When the two brothers got together in Derry, they evidently thought, or came to the conclusion, that they were paying too dearly for the sins of others. With them and their servant in gaol in the month of May [according to press reports all three men were imprisoned at the same time from June onwards with only the farmer imprisoned in May], their farm was being neglected. The result was that, in a day or two after the arrival of the brother and the servant in Derry, I got a letter from the farmer in Derry gaol.

It was addressed to the District Inspector, and as I was acting DI, I opened it along with the other official correspondence. I had already... seen so much and gone through so much that I thought nothing would shock me, but I confess that letter staggered me. Of course, the poor ignorant farmer who wrote it never thought that I would see it. It was a long epistle, but the gist of it was, in short, as follows:

> I told you the day you arrested me who killed Joseph Hayden. I told you that the Specials came to my house and asked me where the Hayden's house was. I am willing to do as much for the cause as either you or Colonel McClintock,

but if you do not have me out of here before Monday, I will tell the whole truth to the military here.

It was clear from this letter that the man had told both my officer and Colonel McClintock who killed Joseph Hayden and wounded his brother and that this man was only in custody as a 'blind' and to save the real murderers. Here was my superior officer clearly guilty of being an accessory after the fact to a felony. What was I, his subordinate, supposed to do? It was horrible to think of it, but after debating it over with my conscience, I concluded that it was best to send it to his superior, the County Inspector. I did so that night but I never saw the letter again.

However, I do know its arrival in Omagh with the County Inspector put the 'wind up', with the result that the District Inspector was ordered to return off leave. The CI came to Cookstown on inspection, and said to me, that was a cool way I sent the letter to him. I had only written a few words on a half sheet of foolscap, saying I was attaching letter received from a prisoner on remand for murder.

I said, 'Yes, I suppose so, but that it was an unusual kind of letter, and that it was not easy to know what to say in submitting such a document.'

He said,

> Yes, but you can see that Mr Hall [George Hall, District Inspector for Cookstown] did not want one police force to be prosecuting another. It will be cleared up in a few days. Colonel McClintock has taken it in hand. We thought at first it was murder, but now we know that it was only manslaughter at most, as Hayden resisted and tried to prevent them from entering the house. And as you know, these men are police just as we are.

The District Inspector returned off leave next day and was ordered to go to Omagh. On his return from Omagh, he came by Tullyhogue and took statements from the 'B' men who were on patrol the night of the murder; the very men he prevented me from arresting the day after the crime was committed. He left the statements on the office table and I read them.

There were five of them, one made by the sergeant of the 'B' men and the others by the 'B' constables who were with him on patrol. The gist of the statements was that they were to search Hayden's house and that the brothers Hayden resisted and wouldn't let them in. They forced an entrance, and when they got inside, Joseph Hayden caught one of their rifles and wouldn't let go. One man admitted shooting him with a revolver, then using his bayonet on both the dead man and his brother.

So here were the admissions of the very men I would have arrested on the day after the murder, had I been permitted. A short time after his return with the statements, he told me to send a man out to warn these murderers, 'witnesses' he called them, to meet him next morning at a place, or places, on the road to Rock. He said, 'I will go to Derry with the "witnesses" myself.'

He went next day with his five 'witnesses' who were to be examined by the competent military authority, but when the military read the statements they converted his 'witnesses' into prisoners. They discharged the farmer, his brother and servant man [according to the press, this did not happen until late August]. He had taken return tickets for his 'witnesses', but had next day to apply for a refund. I really think that this taking of return tickets was done only to fool or deceive the 'B' men, lest they would some day have a shot at himself.

Anyhow, these self-confessed murderers were in Derry gaol when I left Cookstown but some months afterwards I saw where they were allowed out on bail, but I never heard or saw of their being tried for this beastly murder. On the contrary, I did hear that when the wounded man recovered, he was deported out of the Six Counties and had to reside in Monaghan as being a dangerous man. Yet on the day after the crime was committed, the neighbours, both Catholic and Protestant, were loud in their praise of both [Hayden] brothers.[1]

One Protestant neighbour told us it would be impossible to find a more obliging man than Joseph Hayden. After the murder, when the 'B' men got to know that I wanted to charge them with it, I became (if possible) more unpopular. Knowing that the District Inspector was absent and that I was acting DI, they got the idea that they would get me involved in some of their bogus attacks.

Notes

1. None of the 'B' Specials were prosecuted for murder in this case, and it is surprising that they were even charged with it, as the only witness against them was James Hayden, the brother of the murdered man, who was himself seriously wounded. Newspaper reports of the killing give an idea of how it was viewed at the time. The first is from the *Irish News*, Friday 20 May 1921:

MURDER IN TYRONE.
A Catholic Farmer Brutally Killed
Near Cookstown.

HIS BROTHER BADLY WOUNDED
Details of a Shocking Tragedy:
A Motive for the Deed Alleged.
A Cookstown Correspondent wires:

A shocking murder occurred at Gortfad Glebe about five miles from Cookstown, Co. Tyrone, in the early hours of Thursday morning, when the house of Mr. Joseph Hayden was forcibly entered by a gang of men, who are said to have been dressed in police uniforms, armed with rifles and fixed bayonets, and carrying revolvers.

The two brothers, James and Joseph Hayden, who are well known and popular farmers in the locality, live together. The district is almost entirely peopled by Protestants, and the Haydens, who are a Catholic family, lived in peace and friendly intercourse with their neighbours, helping them in all their difficulties.

The facts of the appalling tragedy are as follows: – At about 3.30 a.m. yesterday morning the Hayden brothers were awakened by a knocking at their door, and in answer to his question: "Who's there? James received the reply: " Neighbour". But before he reached the door it was burst open, and the intruders rushed into the bedroom

STABBING HIM THROUGH THE LUNG WITH A BAYONET.

Another member of the band rushed to the bed on which Joseph was, presenting a rifle, which Joseph grasped in an effort to save his life.

The man who had previously bayoneted James came to his comrade's assistance with a loaded revolver, firing and shooting through the abdomen and killing his victim, who was also bayoneted in the head and body.

James Hayden lies in a very critical condition, and Dr. Owens, Pomeroy, who was quickly in attendance, fears he will not recover.

In face of this murder and the many outrages committed in this district by midnight raiders on the homes of the people, an intense feeling of indignation has been aroused in what was heretofore a peaceful locality. It is the confirmed opinion of the supporters of the Anti-Partitionist candidates that this conduct is part of

AN ORGANISED SCHEME TO INTIMIDATE THEM FROM EXPRESSING THEIR FREE WILL AT THE FORTHCOMING ELECTIONS.

Dr. Gillespie,* Coroner for the district, having received intimation of the tragedy from the relatives of the deceased, issued and served his precept on Mr. George Hall, D.I., R.I.C. Cookstown, for the holding of an inquest, whereupon the latter intimated to the Coroner that he had received instructions from the competent military authority that no inquest would be allowed, and that if he the Coroner attempted to hold one he would be processed.

Mr. T.J.S. Harbison M.P. [the Cookstown Nationalist MP for East Tyrone], on behalf of the next-of-kin, joined with the Coroner in emphatically protesting against this action on the part of the military authorities. It is understood a military inquiry will be held today (Friday) in lieu of an inquest.

*This was Doctor James Gillespie, who was also a Sinn Féin activist in the Cookstown area. In a letter to De Valera on 23 November 1921 he was to point out that in his view the Ulster government was 'trying to put down with a mailed fist all who oppose them', having in mind as he did the activities of the Specials in the Cookstown area.

As Eamon Phoenix mentions in his book *Northern Nationalism*, (1994, Ulster Historical Foundation pp. 152–3) the doctor's letter was

> significant as an expression by a Sinn Féin leader at the lack both of effective minority leadership in the north and of any contingency plan for the minority in the event of the continuation of the status quo in Northern Ireland.

Doctor Gillespie would later be interned by the Northern Ireland government on the prison ship *Argenta* in May 1922.

The next report is from the *Newsletter*, Friday 20 May 1921:

BRUTAL TYRONE MURDER.
Farmer Shot Dead in Bed.
HIS BROTHER WOUNDED.

A shocking tragedy occurred at Gortfad Glebe, near Rock, Co. Tyrone, yesterday, when a well-known farmer, Joseph Hayden, was shot dead in bed. His brother, James Hayden, was stabbed through the right lung, and is not expected to recover. The dead man was also found to have been stabbed in the side.

Dominic Hayden, an elder brother, stated that his brothers resided in an adjoining house to his. He was awakened yesterday morning between one and two o'clock by a servant, who said that she heard shooting at his brothers' house. He opened the door, and on looking out saw a man coming down the laneway. The dog attacked a man, who retreated. He then went on to the other house and found that the door had been burst in. His brother James was lying on the floor, and he asked him what had happened. James said that he was badly hurt, but that his brother Joe was shot and was dead. He found that James had been stabbed through the right lung and was in a very weak condition. His brother Joe was lying in bed bleeding freely from a large wound in the right temple. He was then quite dead.

Dr. Owens, Pomeroy, was hastily summoned, and rendered all possible assistance to the injured man, whose position is considered hopeless.

About the same time several men visited the residence of John Daly, Claggan. They demanded a rifle and ordered the entire family of twelve out of their beds. Daly denied that he had a rifle, and then received a severe blow on the right ear with a rifle butt. It is stated he was also stabbed.

District-Inspector Hall and Head-Constable McKenna, with a force of police, subsequently visited Hayden's house. Up to the present, no arrests have been made.

Dr. Gillespie, the coroner for the district, has been informed that a military inquiry will be held in lieu of an inquest.

The *Belfast Telegraph* of Friday 14 May 1921 gave the news of Joseph Hayden's killing under the headlines:

AWFUL TYRONE TRAGEDY

FARMER SHOT DEAD IN BED
BROTHER'S TERRIBLE INJURY
DOG AND SUPPOSED ASSASSIN

The circumstances of the outrage as described by the paper are similar to those described in the *Newsletter*, with the bare facts given. The wording is so alike that it is likely the *Telegraph* and the *Newsletter* correspondents may have shared copy for a good part of their reports.

The *Telegraph* made no suggestion, or offered no description of the perpetrators, saying that the event was 'shrouded in mystery'. The popularity of the Haydens in the district was mentioned, and with 'the news of the tragedy reaching their neighbours they hurried to their assistance from all parts.'

The correspondent wrapped up his report as follows:

Many rumours are current regarding the perpetrators of the murder, but up till the time of wiring no arrests have been made. District Inspector Hall, Cookstown, together with a police platoon, visited the scene yesterday, and are actively investigating the tragedy.

Only the *Irish News* mentioned that the intruders were dressed in police uniform, yet stopped short of saying that they were members of the Special Constabulary

Further reports from the *Tyrone Courier*, Thursday 26 May 1921, shed more light on the circumstances surrounding the killing. The headline was as follows:

MURDER NEAR ROCK
FARMER SHOT DEAD IN BED
HIS BROTHER WOUNDED

The initial description of the crime follows that in the *Irish News* and *Newsletter*, but described the actual killing without naming it as murder:

> Another man, also carrying a rifle, went to the bedroom occupied by Joseph, and leaned over him. Joseph caught the rifle, whereupon the man drew a revolver and shot him dead.

The report also covered the problems which surrounded the military Court of Inquiry into the killing, which was held on Saturday 21 May 1921. Mr J. Hoy, the solicitor, along with Mr T.J.S. Harbinson, MP for the area, '... vigorously protested against the continuation of the inquiry, as the funeral had been arranged for that day.'

The President of the inquiry would not allow solicitors to be present while he took evidence of identification on the remains, which was protested against by Mr Harbinson, who felt that the authorities were attempting to hide something; he insisted that

> ... he, as the local representative in the Imperial Parliament, would see that a proper inquiry was held elsewhere. The people of England would learn of the tragic happenings in that part of the country.

The witnesses and solicitors decided not to take part in the proceedings, with a witness

> ... stating that the nobility were responsible for the present state of the country, as they had been the means of arming irresponsible civilians throughout the district. An armlet and revolver were all that were required.

The President insisted that no burial could place until the remains had been identified.

This corroborated McKenna's memoir when he mentioned the military enquiry taking place on the morning of the funeral, and Mr Hoy the solicitor refusing to co-operate with the enquiry except for identifying the remains.

The report concluded with details of the raid on the home of Mr John Daly of Claggan, which occurred around the same time as the killing of Joseph Hayden.

In the Diary feature (Thursday 16 June 1921) of the *Tyrone Courier* was the following short report:

> Two more arrests have been made in connection with the Hayden murder* – Hugh McMinn, Claggan, brother of the man already accused, and Wm. Devlin, labourer of Gortavale. They have been sent to Derry Jail.

The *Tyrone Courier* edition of Thursday 01 September 1921 described the charging of the Specials with murder:

THE HAYDEN TRAGEDY
SPECIAL CONSTABLES ACCUSED
Their Story At Enquiry

The events which took place at a special court in Derry on Wednesday August 31 were described, when

> six members of the "B" class Special Constabulary ... were charged with the murder of Joseph Hayden, Gortfad. There was an alternative charge of manslaughter ... Sergeant Young (Derry) said he arrested the accused on 29th June. They made no statement.

A description of the events on the early hours of 19 May 1921 was given again, but also present were some details regarding evidence which McKenna gives in his memoir. Additional evidence in the form of pipes found at the scene further highlight poor RIC practice when they did not at least attempt to link members of the raiding party with any of the four articles found.

> Thomas Hayden, another brother, gave evidence of finding an article in the house which police described as an oil bottle. He had never seen a bottle like it before, and neither of his brothers had a rifle or oil bottle. He also found two pipes, one under the bed in which Joseph was, and the other on the opposite side of the room.

*Here the slaying is named as 'murder'.

Edward Falls, J.P., Drumballyhue, said Dominick Hayden called for him early that morning and he went with him to the house. On the pathway between the road and Hayden's house, a piece of a rifle was found.

Cuthbert H. Tomb, a member of the "B" Special Constabulary, said he was one of "Hutchinson's squad". On the night of the 18th, or the morning of the 19th May, they were raiding for illegal arms ... Later, he heard a shot, and on entering the house he saw a man whom he did not know struggling with two of the patrol for a rifle. He saw another man striking at one of the patrol. The only light in the house was Hutchinson's flash lamp, and it became broken. The two men were in their night attire. When the light went out the specials came out of the house.

Lieut.-Colonel Eaves, Derry, said he held a preliminary investigation for the purpose of taking down a summary of evidence in connection with the homicide of Joseph Hayden. The accused subsequently signed the summaries. No threat or inducement was used against the prisoners at the inquiry.

The court was adjourned to enable the solicitor for the defence to see the summaries.

Later it appeared that the statements of the six accused as witnesses at the preliminary military investigation of the charges against the two McMinns and Devlin were to the effect that on instructions they raided Hayden's house for arms. When they knocked a voice said, "Who's there?" 'They replied, "Special police come to search for arms." The voice inside said, "We won't let you in here." Hutchinson said, "We are not coming to do you any harm, and if you don't let us in we will have to break in the door. " They waited ten minutes and, as the door was not opened, they burst it in. William Jordan was knocked down by a man, believed to be James Hayden, who stooped to pick up Jordan's rifle. Several of the accused pushed Hayden away into the bedroom, and Hutchinson's revolver was knocked on the bed. Joseph Hayden, who was sitting on the side of the bed, picked up the revolver. A struggle for possession of the weapon ensued, and a shot was discharged harmlessly. Joseph Hayden then seized hold of Duncan Jordan's rifle, and pressed the trigger several times, but as the safety catch

Katie and John around about the time they got married, c. 1898.

Katie Byrne, John McKenna's wife-to-be, contemplates married life, *c.* 1898.

could do better, & That I'm sure is true, but does wealth always bring happiness Mine. I know is an humble position but it may be better. There is no stain on my character, so that I have a chance to compete for promotion if I wish writing about my position reminds me of your promotion, which Katie told me of this morning. so I now beg to(?) congratulate you. In conclusion I again ask you to grant me the favour which I have asked. and I hope that when you consider the temper I was in when I wrote that letter, that you wont think so badly of me If you could only imagine yourself to be in the same position as I am in & know how dearly I love Katie I'm sure you wouldn't be so hard on us
      I am Yours Respectfully
            Jno McKenna

John McKenna on the brink of betrothal – the early days in Galway.
From a letter to Laurence dated 30 September 1896,
quoted in the Family Background section.

Mazy had a letter and a new Gown She made in good S— for the races. McKenna's Sister is come to stay and learn the trade for 12 mo. all doing well and getting good health herself and John Mc w'd have been at Tuam Races only that two of the men went on duty to the North for the 12th of July where it was feared that disturbeince would take place

I am My very dear Laurence Your fond Father
Jas Byrne

L. J. Byrne Esq

John McKenna's father-in-law mentions the young constable missing out on Tuam Races owing to having to cover for colleagues being posted north for the Twelfth of July (*c.* 1898); quoted in Family Background.

DEATHS.

CURRID—May 20, at Cloonaghcrin, County Sligo, Annie Currid, relict of the late James Currid, of Cloonaghcrin, and mother of Patrick Currid, R.I.C., Ballymena.

M'KENNA—May 23, 1905, at her parents' residence, Henry Street, Florence Mary (Baba), darling child of Constable and Mrs. M'Kenna, aged 4 years.—R.I.P.

Death notice in the *Ballymena Observer*, 26 May 1905 for John McKenna's young daughter, Florence Mary.

DEATH OF FLORENCE MARY M'KENNA.

Much regret was experienced in Harryville on Tuesday last when the sad intelligence of the death of the above child, daughter of Constable and Mrs. M'Kenna, of Henry Street, became known. The deceased was a bright and winsome little girl, and was a particular favourite with all who knew her. She had been ailing for some time past having had an attack of measles, followed by other complications. She was skilfully attended by Dr. R. Currie and Dr. W. R. Davison, but despite everything that medical science and careful and tender nursing on a fond loving mother's part she passed calm and tranquilly away into a sunnier clime on Tuesday last. Much sympathy is evinced on the part of everyone with the grief-stricken parents in the great bereavement which has fallen upon them.

The remains of the deceased were removed from her father's residence on Wednesday evening last for interment in the burial ground connected with Crebilly R.C. Church, and were followed to their last resting place by a large concourse of people, including all the available sergeants and men of the two barracks. Beautiful wreaths and other floral tributes were sent by the men of the Harryville barrack, the men of the High Street barrack, one from the father and mother, one from Mrs. P. Deighan, Galgorm Street, and flowers from Miss Lavender, Mrs Williams, Miss Taylor, and Mrs. M'Cullough. Mr. Bernard Laird, Larne St., had charge of the funeral arrangements, and the hearse and mourning carriages were supplied by Mr. J. Fleming, Queen Street.

Obituary from paper of same date. This glowing tribute to the passing of a beloved child also provides some insight into the RIC barracks in Ballymena and the esteem in which John McKenna was held.

I send you the paper, Mary, which gives a short account of her death. Again, Mary, I thank you, and Laurence, on my own, and my husband's behalf, for your very great kindness and trusting God may bless you both,

I am My dear Mary

Your devoted Sister

Katie

Part of a letter from Katie McKenna to her sister-in-law Mary Byrne (mentioned in the Family Background section). She mentions sending the *Ballymena Observer* which reports the death of her and John's four year old child Florence. See previous page for this report.

Outside the Barracks in Carnlough, 1911. Katie and John with their two youngest children (at that time), Rose (left) and Pauline (right). Rose would die in a matter of months after this photo was taken. Pauline is about 2 years old, and died on 16 February 2009 in her one hundredth year.

The 1911 census return for the McKenna family, with Sergeant McKenna omitted due to his being on the barracks return. See photograph on previous page taken outside the family home (to the rear of the barracks) around this time.

CENSUS OF IRELAND, 1911.

Form H.—Return of Military, R. I. Constabulary or Metropolitan Police, in Barracks.

County: Antrim   Parliamentary Division: Mid Antrim   Poor Law Union: Larne   District Electoral Division: Solarbrie   Townland: ____   No. on Form B: 1

Parliamentary Borough: ____   Urban District: ____   City: ____   Town or Village: Carnlough, Main Street, Harbour Road

GENERAL RETURN of the Officers, Non-Commissioned Officers, Privates, and Others, who were Quartered in the R. I. Constabulary Barrack of Carnlough on the Night of Sunday, the 2nd of April, 1911, and of those who arrived on Monday, the 3rd of April, who were not enumerated elsewhere.

Initial Letters of Christian Name or Names & of Surname		RANK.	RELIGIOUS PROFESSION.	EDUCATION.	AGE.	OCCUPATION.	MARRIAGE.	WHERE BORN.	IRISH LANGUAGE.
Christian Name	Surname								
J. M'K.	M'K.	Sergeant R.I.C.	Roman Catholic	Read & write	39	Farmer Son	Married	Co. Monaghan	
J. D.	D.	Constable R.I.C.	Church of Ireland	"	23	do	Single	Co. Cavan	
W. G.	G.	Constable R.I.C.	Roman Catholic	"	23	do	Single	Co. Roscommon	Irish & English

John McKenna's return for Carnlough Barracks, written in his own hand in his role as census enumerator. It is possible that the Church of Ireland constable was the one deputised by the District Inspector to find out how many Ulster Volunteers were in the village.

John is fourth from the left in the front row. He was posted to Kildare in
1921 prior to disbandment at the Curragh in 1922.

The recently retired Head Constable relaxes
at his brother-in-law Laurence's house,
London *c*. 1925.

John with his sister, Ellen Sexton, his son Peter and Ellen's daughter Mary, *c.* 1925.

John with his 3 surviving sons, Larne *c.* 1930; Peter (the editor's father), stands behind him, with Tony (Patrick) on the left, and Teddy (John) seated. John's wife Katie passed away in 1929, probably not long before this picture was taken. Tony is now 91.

John with his sister Ellen and daughter Aileen, with sons Tony and Peter at the back, Larne c. 1930.

At the back are Mary Jo (daughter), John, Pauline (daughter), Teddy (son) and Madeleine (daughter). In front of them are Mary Sexton (niece), Ellen Sexton (sister), and Aileen (daughter). At the very front is Tony (son), Larne c. 1930.

John the family man. At the back are his niece, Mary Sexton and his daughter Aileen. In the middle, his daughters Madeline and Pauline, son Tony and his sister Ellen Sexton. Standing a little apart is his eldest daughter Mary Jo. The young girl is Helen Fearon, the daughter of a family friend, Kilkeel 1932.

From left, Ellen Sexton (sister), Brian McGuckian (son-in-law who married John's daughter Pauline) with Mary (Brian's daughter and John's granddaughter) in his arms; Mary Sexton (niece) and John, Larne 1936.

Unknown male, Tom Sexton (brother-in-law),
John and Ellen Sexton (sister), *c.* 1936.

John pictured during a visit to St Macartan's, Monaghan, to see his daughter Kathleen *c.* 1940.

John is pictured here with 4 of his daughters and his first grandchild, Mary. The 3 nuns are Madeline (Sister Mary Paula), Sadie (Sister Mary Emilian) and Kathleen (Sister Mary Comgall), with Pauline, Mary's mother, the late Mrs McGuckian. St Macartan's, Monaghan *c.* 1940.

Also at St Macartan's: John, 4 daughters and granddaughter Mary, *c.* 1940.

John, Tony (son), Ellen Sexton (sister), Teddy (son) and Mary Sexton (niece), Larne *c.* 1940.

THE IRISH TIMES, MONDAY, JUNE 27, 1932.

HISTORIC SCENE IN THE PHŒNIX PARK.

THE FIFTEEN ACRES.	TREMENDOUS CONGREGATION HEARS MASS.	UGLY SCENES IN THE NORTH
A VAST OPEN-AIR CHURCH.	POSSIBLE NEW CARDINAL.	THE MIGHTY INVASION.	MOBS ATTACK PILGRIMS.
HOW THE CROWD FELT.	DR. BYRNE'S NAME SUGGESTED.	ALL NATIONALITIES AND ALL ORDERS REPRESENTED.	HOW IRELAND CAME TO DUBLIN.	WOMEN ROUGHLY HANDLED.
MILLION MINDS WITH A SINGLE THOUGHT.				TRAIN BOMBARDED WITH STONES.

STEAMER PILGRIMS

PASS THROUGH FUSILADE OF STONES.

Pilgrims en route for the Eucharistic Congress in Dublin were attacked by a mob while marching to board a steamer at Larne.

Two omnibuses, carrying elderly people from a Roman Catholic Church Service arrived at the steamer with nothing but the window frames on one side of the 'bus, while some of the passengers had cuts on their faces.

The main procession of pilgrims was pelted on the way to the quay, several people being struck with the stones.

Two motor cars, one of them with a priest as passenger, went through a fusillade of stones.

An attempt was made to rush the gangway.

An attempt to snatch a Eucharistic banner from its bearer was checked by the police, but was followed by stone-throwing at the passengers on the steamer.

Women took shelter behind the bulwarks. One or two men received nasty blows on the face.

Windows and portholes on the steamer were broken, and even as the vessel steamed out volley after volley of stones landed upon her decks.

Bishop Daniel Mageean of Down and Connor who also attended the Eucharistic Congress. Mentioned by John McKenna as 'our beloved Bishop' he conducted correspondence in the pages of the *Irish News* with Dawson Bates, Northern Ireland Minister of Home Affairs, in the summer of 1932 (see p. 4 of the Eucharistic Congress section and details of actual correspondence on pp. 8–10).

Images (top and above right) showing headlines from the *Irish Times*, Monday 27 June 1932, recording the historic scenes taking place in Phoenix Park, coupled with the attacks on pilgrims in the north. Reproduced courtesy of the *Irish Times*.

Daniel O'Connell's statue oversees the fruits of Catholic Emancipation as multitudes assemble in the centre of Dublin from all over the world for the Eucharistic Congress, June 1932. Photograph reproduced from *Thirty First International Eucharistic Congress Dublin, 1932,* courtesy of Veritas, Dublin.

Deaths

HALL (Belfast)—April 13, 1943, at the City Hospital, John, youngest son of Thomas and Kathleen Hall. Funeral from 19 Osman Street to-day (Wednesday), at 2.30 p.m., to Milltown Cemetery.
Deeply regretted by his Daddy and Mammy, and Relatives.

KELLY (Belfast)—April 12, 1943, at her residence, 42 Torrens Crescent, Ellen (Nellie), dearly-beloved wife of Alexander Kelly.—R.I.P. Funeral from above address on to-day (Wednesday), at 2 p.m., to Milltown Cemetery.
On her soul, sweet Jesus, have mercy. Inserted by her sorrowing Husband and Family.

KELLY (Belfast)—April 12, 1943, at her residence, 42 Torrens Crescent, Ellen (Nellie), dearly-beloved daughter of Elizabeth Steele and the late James Steele.—R.I.P. Funeral from above address on to-day (Wednesday), at 2 p.m., to Milltown Cemetery.
St. Ann, pray for her.
Deeply regretted by her sorrowing Mother, and Sister, Elizabeth.
18 New Lodge Road.

MILLEN (Belfast)—April 12, 1943, at Purdysburn Fever Hospital, Ellen (aged 7 years), dearly-beloved daughter of James and Margaret Millen. Her remains will be removed from the above Hospital on to-day (Wednesday), at 11.30 a.m., passing Beechfield Street at 12 o'clock for interment in Milltown Cemetery.
Deeply regretted by her Father, Mother, Brothers and Sisters.
69 Beechfield Street.

MacLAVERTY—At St. John's Nursing Home, Belfast, 13th April, 1943, Rev. John A. MacLaverty, Administrator of St. Peter's, Belfast. Solemn Office and Requiem Mass in St. Peter's Pro-Cathedral on to-morrow (Thursday, 15th April), at 11 a.m.

McELVOGUE (Aghadowey, Co. Derry)—April 13, 1943, at her residence, Corramuckla, Aghadowey, Mary A. McElvogue.—R.I.P. Funeral to Mullamore Burying-ground on to-morrow (Thursday, 15th), following Requiem Mass at St. Mary's R.C. Church, Aghadowey.
Deeply regretted by her sorrowing Family, Bill, May, Kathleen and Jim, also her Sisters, E. and S. Mooney, 21 Fruithill Park, Belfast.

McKENNA (Belfast)—April 12, 1943 (suddenly), at his residence, 43 Rushfield Avenue, Hugh Leo—R.I.P. beloved husband of Winifred (Una) McKenna. Requiem Mass in Holy Rosary Church at 9 o'clock to-day (Wednesday). Funeral immediately afterwards to Milltown Cemetery. No flowers by request.
Sacred Heart of Jesus, have mercy on his soul.
Deeply regretted by his loving Wife and Family.

McKENNA (Larne)—April 13, 1943, John McKenna (ex Head-Constable, R.I.C.), Bay Road, Larne Harbour, father of Sister M. Emelian, Carrickmacross, Sister M. Comgall, Monaghan, and Sister M. Paula, Ballymena, Sisters of St. Louis. Remains will be removed to St. MacNissi's, Larne, this (Wednesday) evening, at 6 o'clock. Requiem Mass at 8.30, and funeral to Crebilly on to-morrow (Thursday), at 11 o'clock. May he rest in peace.

McMANUS (Belfast)—April 13, 1943, at her residence, 154 Cromac Street, Ellen, dearly-beloved wife of Thomas McManus.—R.I.P. Her remains will be removed to St. Malachy's R.C. Church, Alfred Street, this (Wednesday) evening, at 8 o'clock.
On her soul, sweet Jesus, have mercy.
Deeply regretted by her sorrowing Husband and Family.

McVEIGH—March 15, 1943, at Birmingham, Patrick McVeigh—R.I.P.—(late of 51 Hawthorn Street, Belfast).
Good St. Anne, pray for him.
Deeply regretted by his sorrowing Daughter, Elizabeth, and Son-in-law, Patrick Evans; also his Sons, Patrick and Francis.

Acknowledgments

The Family of the late John Kearney wish to return their sincere thanks to all those who sympathised with them in their recent sad bereavement.
40 McCleery Street.

KEITH—The Relatives of the late Victoria Keith wish to thank all those who sympathised with them in their recent bereavement, particularly those who sent Mass cards.
28 Newington Avenue.

In Memoriam

COSTELLO (Third Anniversary)—In loving memory of Peter, who died 14th April, 1940; also his two children.

BELFAST MORNING NEWS
Pro Fide et Patria

Offices:	Telephones:
Belfast...113-117 Donegall Street	Belfast 25486
London....177-178 Fleet Street	London .... Central 8497
Glasgow... 21 Hope Street, C.2.	Glasgow .... Central 2290

WEDNESDAY, APRIL 14, 1943.   ST. JUSTIN, M.

An Oft-Told Tale

PERIODICALLY since the outbreak of war Unionists have announced that their desire to maintain a political truce has been frustrated by their opponents, who never ceased to avail of an opportunity to assail "Ulster's" position. Because of these opponents it had been found necessary, they declare, to resume their activities as in pre-war days.

We do not know how often this tale has been told. But it is told once again in the report to be presented to the "Ulster" Unionist Council on Friday. The resumption of party enterprise is deplored. "This step may be regarded as regrettable in war time," states the report, "but" it adds melodramatically, "when the 'Ulster' Constitution is attacked Unionists must meet the challenge."

We may read into this fresh resolve an apology for lost battles. It is over two years since the official party was defeated in North Down, and the excuse was that the political machinery was not working so well as it used to do because the organisation was too busy helping to win the war. It is almost a year and a half since the party was defeated in Willowfield, and an attempt was then made to explain the result away with more talk about the elusive truce, which handicapped the party.

It is two months since the party was defeated in West Belfast, and once again comes the story that "comparatively little attention was paid to party politics since the outbreak of war." Is it not about time this threadbare legend was forsaken, since even the Unionist rank and file know that it is incompetence and maladministration, and not patriotic concentration on the war effort, that is responsible for election reverses and internal strife?

But if such an authority is to be effective discussion on it cannot take place too early or too often, and however little the people's faith in such an instrument as a means of preserving the peace of the world after the failure of the League of Nations, some such means will be required when the war ends if the world is to be spared the suffering of recurring wars. It is the only hope of it being so spared, and the greater the firmness of its establishment the greater its promise. That firmness will come only by

executors of the estate of Eliza Jane Richie, with with having obtained that sum from the Munster and Leinster Bank, Belfast, by false pretences.
Glover was also charged with forging a bank draft endorsement in favour of Elizabeth Jane M'Clune. Gordon was charged with aiding and abetting.

D.-I.'s EVIDENCE.

District-Inspector Murphy, prosecuting, said that Gordon would also be charged with bigamy and Glover with having aided and abetted.
The D.-I. stated that a bank draft for Elizabeth Jane M'Aloncy of 97a Cupar Street, for £58 8s 6d from the will of her aunt in Iowa, had been intercepted by the

---

John's own death notice reflects both the strong Catholicism of his family and the ties with the family burial plot near Ballymena where children Florence, James, Rose and his wife Katie were already buried.

Ex-Head Constable.

THE death took place in a Belfast nursing home on Tuesday of Mr. John M'Kenna, Bay Road, Larne, an ex-head constable of the R.I.C., who had formerly been stationed here, and came to reside in the town when he completed his police service. Mr. M'Kenna had not been too well recently, but the end came suddenly, to the great regret of the legion of friends that his kindly and genial personality gained for him. Mr. M'Kenna was a native of Co. Monaghan, and after serving as a constable in East Galway and Ballymena, he was promoted sergeant and sent to Carnlough, afterwards coming to Larne, where he also carried out the duties of weights and measures inspector. With promotion to head-constable he was transferred to Kenmare (Co. Kerry), and later he served in Cookstown and Kildare, where he finished 30 years' service. Mr. M'Kenna's wife predeceased him some years ago. He was a devout Roman Catholic and every morning attended early mass at St. MacNissi's. Three of his six daughters are Nuns—Sisters of St. Louis, and the others are Mrs. Brian M'Guigan, Cloughmills; Miss Mary J. M'Kenna, P.E. School teacher at Garron Point; and Miss Eileen M'Kenna, a nurse in London. He is also survived by three sons — Peter, Terry, and Tony. The last-named is a Sergt.-Observer in the R.A.F., and only recently returned from Canada where he did his air-crew training.

This obituary from the *Larne Times* of Thursday 15 April 1943 shows again the esteem in which John was held during his lifetime. A dedicated Catholic and family man, only his son Tony is alive today. After the War he would follow in his father's footsteps and join the police (in London).

10th August, 1914

Dear Sergeant McKenna,

A large number of your friends and well-wishers in Carnlough have thought that the occasion of your transfer to Larne gave a favourable opportunity for marking the esteem in which you have been held during the years of your residence amongst them. We, therefore, beg to tender to you the hearty thanks of the community for your courteous and efficient discharge of your duties, and wish you and Mrs. McKenna many years of success and happiness. On behalf of the residents of all creeds and classes, we beg to ask you to accept this address and the accompanying purse of sovereigns.

With sincere good wishes, we are, on behalf of the subscribers, yours very faithfully,

Joseph Burns, P.P.
Jas. Foster, J.P.
Thos. Logan, J.P.

To Sergeant McKenna,
R.I.C.
Larne.

The presentation which was made to John McKenna after his departure to Larne from Carnlough in 1914 gives no hint of the turmoil which the unexpected move caused him. Nevertheless, it is a fitting testimonial from both sides of the community as to his integrity as a police officer.

was locked, it did not go off. The raiding party afterwards retired, leaving the Haydens all right.

The accused were remanded on bail until Friday, 9th September when James Hayden's deposition will be taken at his own home.

The evidence at the earlier investigation was contradicted by the *Courier*'s report in the aftermath of the killing, when it was stated that Joseph Hayden was killed with a revolver at the time of the Specials raid, not at some later unspecified occasion.

The statements taken from the Specials (information relating to subsequent proceedings against them mention six, not five Specials in total, as McKenna said) by DI George Hall resulted from McKenna's passing of the letter from the farmer neighbour to the County Inspector. They were dated 11 June.

What they each had in common was a specific statement that neither the neighbouring farmer, his manservant and his brother were present at the scene of the crime, even though James Hayden placed Devlin (the servant) as definitely being there. The farmer's threat to tell the truth about who killed Joseph (as mentioned in the letter McKenna intercepted) had borne fruit, in that the Specials went out of their way to state that the farmer, his brother or the manservant had not been present at the scene of the shooting. This was presumably the price of their agreeing not to name the killers. McKenna states categorically in his memoir that the killing was described and admitted to, yet the statements held in the Public Record Office of Northern Ireland (PRONI file HA/5/161 'Relating to proposed prosecution of 'B' Specials for the murder of Joseph Hayden, Co. Tyrone') do not show this. Either McKenna was mistaken or they were tampered with after he saw them in order to minimise the deeds of the Specials.

The statements described how the Haydens allegedly reacted aggressively to the raid, with Joseph apparently succeeding in wresting a revolver from the Sergeant, then pointing it at him. According to one of the Specials' statements, he managed to take a rifle from a Constable, and would have killed the Sergeant had the safety catch not been on. This statement was mentioned in the *Tyrone Courier* report of 01 September 1921.

James was also alleged to have been shouting 'Fight on, Joe' as encouragement to fight back. A Constable further claimed that

> When the revolver went off I did not know that anyone had been hit. The man who is dead went on fighting and said nothing about being wounded.

The Specials claimed to have left both brothers alive and uninjured. One of the Constables stated that 'we made no search for weapons as far as I know.' The reason given for not conducting a search was that their searchlights had been broken in the brawl.

A Special Constable who was not inside the house at the time of the raid also made a statement which seemed to contradict the claims of those who would be arrested and later charged. He mentioned going inside and witnessing the struggle. 'I did not know that anyone was injured till I came out. Then I went in again and heard that he was shot.' His was the only acknowledgement in a Specials' statement that Joseph had been shot.

James Hayden's deposition in respect of the Specials' trial was taken at his home in Gortfad on Friday 9 September 1921, and was reported in the *Irish News* of 10 September 1921:

> The depositions of Mr James Hayden were taken seated on a chair beside his bed. He is in a very delicate state of health.

The Specials' claim that the Haydens tried to physically resist their entry on the night of Joseph's murder was called into question, as James said that

> "... I opened the door. It was very dark then. As soon as the door was opened there came a rush of men into the kitchen. I was struck on the left temple with the butt of a rifle. The blow on the temple knocked me back into the bedroom."

James Hayden mentioned his brother grabbing hold of a rifle (held by William Devlin) from the bed, but did not suggest that Joe had grabbed and attempted to fire a revolver or rifle as previously suggested by the Specials. Rather than saying 'fight on, Joe', as the Specials had claimed, James stated that he said,

> "Joe, let it go and let them go their way. Don't bother your head with them." Then a man standing between Hugh McMinn and Jeremiah McMinn – this man drew a revolver from his side and deliberately shot my brother. My brother got up slightly on the bed, leaned backwards with his head on the window, and died on the spot.

James himself was then bayoneted at the back of his right shoulder, and

> knew nothing more until my brothers Dominick and Thomas arrived. I knew none of the men save the three I have mentioned.

Although the neighbouring farmer, his brother and the servant Devlin were charged with Joseph Hayden's murder, it was inevitable that a trial would not proceed. As no one other than James had placed any of the three at the scene a trial would have been futile. James failed to identify any of the

Specials as being there, although he recognised one of them as a neighbour.

Under the late news column of the *Tyrone Courier* of Thursday 25 August 1921 was the following:

THE HAYDEN TRAGEDY
Three Civilians Released

The three civilians Jeremiah McMinn and Hugh McMinn, Crossdernott, and William Devlin, Gortavale, Rock, who were arrested in May last in connection with the shooting of Joseph Hayden, Gortfad, and have since been imprisoned in Derry Jail were released on Tuesday evening.

On Wednesday an application was to have been made to the High Court of Justice, Dublin, for a writ of habeas corpus in respect of the three men. The necessary affadavits were made and filed on their behalf, whereupon the Government directed their release, the authorities intimating they considered on the evidence obtained the men were not guilty.

> In his statement in respect of the McMinn case the Specials Sergeant stated that the only shot fired in the bedroom that night did not hit anyone, and that they left 'the two Haydens in their bedroom, as far as I know unhurt.'
>
> He also said that five members of his unit took home weapons unchecked by him (checking them for usage was required by regulations) at the end of the night. As only two of these unit members with unchecked weapons were among the Specials at the house that night, the Sergeant implied that someone else could have visited the Haydens after the raid. Another Special admitted that 'our men's rifles had bayonets in them in the bedroom'.
>
> The *Tyrone Courier* in the edition of 25 August 1921 also carried a small report on damages being claimed under the heading:

THE HAYDEN TRAGEDY

Margaret Hayden, of Gortfad, Glebe, claimed for the murder of her son Joseph Hayden, on 19th May £5,000.

James Hayden, of Gortfad, Glebe, claimed £5,000 for malicious injuries on 19th May.

> In September 1921 the six Specials were returned for trial to the next assizes, the Winter Assizes in Belfast. This was then deferred until the Tyrone Assizes. An intriguing tale developed at this point which directly involved

the Ministry of Home Affairs, part of the fledgling administration of the new state. A mother of one of the 'B' men (a nineteen year old) penned a letter to the Ministry, railing against the perceived injustice of her son and his colleagues being in prison. Addressed to Sir James Craig, the Prime Minister, the lady referred indignantly to a postponement of the trial from Belfast to the next Assizes in Tyrone.

This postponement came about because of the unavailability of a 'material witness' for the Belfast Assizes. The material witness was James Hayden, who had not been expected to live in the immediate aftermath of the shooting. His Doctor had provided a medical certificate stating he was unfit to travel to Belfast from Tyrone for the trial, which had led to it being put back to the Spring Assizes in Tyrone in the New Year.

The Special's mother saw this as part of a plot designed to see her son and the others convicted, possibly under a Free State government. At the time, the Boundary Commission provided for in the Anglo-Irish Treaty of 1921 was still pending, and it was by no means certain (at least to ordinary people) that Tyrone would remain in Northern Ireland.

> Now I think you will agree with me if our country should be destined to go under the Southern Parliament what fair play can we expect in a case such as this?

The concerned mother further elaborated that the medical certificate was 'signed by an RC Doctor', and in her view was therefore suspect, particularly as she asserted that James Hayden had been seen going about his business as normal. The letter was dated 20 December 1921.

Today we would expect such a letter to be treated with extreme caution, but the Northern Ireland Cabinet took it very seriously. An official in the department of Home Affairs did not think it unlikely that the medical certificate was bogus and gave instructions that the matter be investigated. If this could be proven, then they would see about getting the case transferred back to Belfast. This memo was dated 23 December 1921. 'I plead with you in God's name and in the name of justice that you and your honourable Cabinet see to it that those boys are released', the mother went on. She is secure in the knowledge that her 19 year old son has, 'from his earliest childhood, only stood for what was noble and right.' The lady in question may have been a person of some influence, as she appeared confident of a favourable outcome. 'I leave it with you – can such treatment tend to make loyal citizens?'

Perhaps this letter and the reaction to it goes some way towards explaining why the new Northern Ireland administration would not countenance members of the Special Constabulary being tried for murder, much less found guilty of it. The Attorney General in the north directed a *Nolle Prosequi* (a decision not to proceed with the case), which was needless, on 04 January 1922, because a 'True Bill has not been found', as stated by the Crown Solicitor, James Riordan (still based in Dublin at that time) on 16

January 1922. The defendants' Solicitor was advised by Riordan that 'it is not the intention of the Crown to proceed further with the case.' Other entries in the file mentioned there being no chance of the Crown successfully prosecuting the Specials due to lack of evidence.

Of course, the true extent of any cover-up is now impossible to ascertain, but the Haydens were a respectable family, and at the time, neither the *Irish News* nor *Newsletter* reports of the killing left any doubt that it had been cold-blooded murder. A *Tyrone Courier* report from the edition dated 26 May 1921 stated that

> The Haydens are all very popular in the neighbourhood, and are well-known Constitutional Nationalists holding, it is said, very strong and outspoken views antagonistic to Sinn Féin.

James Hayden was the only witness who could realistically have testified against the Specials, and if he had died after the attack (as was expected), there would have been no case to answer.

A trial of the Specials may have been futile, particularly as we see from the memoir that no effort was made to place any of them at the scene of the crime. There was no following up of evidence, such as the rifle stock and oil bottle found in the vicinity of the murder. There is no doubt that the Specials in Tyrone were out of control that night, and were not accompanied by an RIC officer, as was supposed to be the case. A letter is on the PRONI file supporting this, being addressed by the RIC Divisional Commissioner based in Belfast to the Tyrone County Commandant in Omagh. It was dated 28 May 1921, only a few weeks after the slaying of Joseph Hayden.

> Ref. to your letter 1254 of 27th Inst., I am applying to the I.G. (Inspector General) for legal aid in the case to be heard on the 2nd June.
>
> I would, however, point out that I consider the action of these B men in carrying out searches on their own without any application to the Permanent Police is highly undesirable.
>
> I am not satisfied that the B men of this district are sufficiently under control, and I request that you will take immediate steps to see that their actions are controlled, and that they are brought in close touch with the Permanent Police. Anything in the shape of partisan action will bring discredit on the Force, and will be exceedingly difficult to justify in a court of law when the opposition are represented by trained legal advisors.

The RIC Commissioner's clear concern at the undisciplined activities of the Ulster Special Constabulary was shared by the British government's representative S.G. Tallents in 1922, but James Craig, Northern Ireland Prime Minister, stoutly defended the force he had helped to create. McKenna's concerns about the lack of fair play for Catholics in 1932 were foreshadowed by his direct experience as Head Constable in Cookstown at the onset of partition in 1921. Northern nationalists would always be under suspicion in the eyes of the Unionist government. They were, in the words of Sir Basil Brooke in 1933, '99 per cent disloyal.'

The killing of a man widely respected in his community made concerns about the activities of the Specials all the more pertinent. The *Ulster Herald* of Saturday 28 May 1921 covered the aftermath of the killing under the heading:

THE FUNERAL

The funeral, which took place to Tullyodonnel Chapel, was the largest ever seen in the district and was representative of all creeds and classes bearing ample testimony to the esteem in which the deceased was held. Long before the hour of removal large crowds of mourners wended their way along the road to deceased's home, and all were horror-stricken on examining the bed and room where deceased met so brutal and cruel an end.

The homily at the Mass, which was celebrated by Rev. J. Mackin, mentioned that the

deceased was a good quiet man who gave no offence or provocation to anyone and did not take part in politics, he simply attended to his work and bothered no-one, living a good and quiet life, but his was not a quiet death waking up in the middle of the night to face the dagger of the assassin.

Father Mackin also 'hoped that the authorities would do the utmost that could be done to bring the perpetrators to justice', that 'no stone would be left unturned.'

McKenna too would have shared that hope, but even as a Head Constable of the RIC found that he was powerless to bring it about.

'Running Amok':
McAdoo's Car

On the following Sunday, I went out at about 12 midnight. Everything was quiet, but I was scarcely asleep when the guard came and informed me that there was some shooting up the town. I got up and roused all the men, and going outside, could hear of nothing being wrong. The shots had evidently been fired as a signal for the 'B' men to assemble, as a regular army of them had assembled near the barracks.

In a few minutes a motor cyclist from Tullyhogue arrived breathless, and throwing himself off the bike shouted out 'We were attacked!' He pretended to be so excited he could hardly deliver his message, which was that the Tullyhogue 'B' patrol (the same section to which the patrol that killed Joe Hayden belonged) was attacked at Annaghmore.

I had no alternative but to get out the cars and go to Annaghmore, although I knew well from the way the 'B' men had already turned out with their motors in such numbers that the whole thing was 'staged.' Having got the Crossley car out and filled it with Specials and one RIC man, I proceeded to Annaghmore accompanied by the cyclist who reported the attack. When we got to the place, I told the driver to pull up.

It was a most unlikely place for an ambush, and if I were an officer of the supposed enemy I would certainly have the man who planned an attack in such a place court martialled. It was a flat district, the only cover being sod fences. The 'B' men were lying on the side of the road along a low sod fence. I asked them where the attackers were, but without answering they shouted, get down, or you'll be shot. I got down, and again asked where the attack came from.

They pointed over a flat field to a low fence on the other side of it about 100 yards distant and said, 'over there'. There being no sign of activity amongst the imaginary enemy, and knowing that the whole thing was bogus, I thought of a ruse for getting them away from the place.

I said to them that the real attack might be on Rock Barrack and that the shooting at Annaghmore might only be done as a 'blind' to keep us engaged while they (the enemy) might at that moment be attacking Rock. They made no reply, so I said to the driver, 'Drive on to Rock', and got the men into the car and proceeded to the barracks.

We had only got a few hundred yards when, on passing a farm house on the same side of the road from where the alleged attack had come, one of the Specials in the car suggested that we make enquiry of the farmer, who was only a few yards from the road in front of the house, as to whether he had seen the enemy. I agreed and pulled up. The Special who had made the suggestion jumped out of the car, accompanied by another, and ran up to the farmer and spoke to him.

They had only just spoken to him and I had only just got out of the car, when the Special who suggested we should stop, shouted 'this way, this way', to the men in the car and started to run behind the farmer's house. I shouted at them to halt and they did so. I then went up to the farmer and asked him what information he had given the Special. He said that he had given no information, as he had none to give. He said he knew nothing about what we were after.[1]

It was evident that the Specials wanted to get out of my control and run amok when they got out of my sight, so I ordered them into the car and we proceeded to Rock Barrack. It was then about 1.30 am. I knocked and got Sergeant Gallagher, whom I told about the alleged attack and what I thought about it. I told him I had only called there in order to get away from the plot and that he could go back to his bed.

I then started on the return journey to Cookstown, but we were only about a mile out of Rock when we met a motor car with powerful headlights. It pulled up as we met it, and out of it jumped the

Cookstown 'B' Head Constable, Sidney McClelland, the confederate of my own District Inspector, whom I then, and now, believe was the organiser of the staged attack. He had three or four cartridges in his hand, and holding them up to me said, this is some of the stuff they were using; flat-nosed expanding bullets.

I asked him where they were found, and he said, in the field behind the ditch ... I handed the bullets back to him and asked him if the other 'B' men had gone home. He said no, they had gone up to Movea, that the Movea Road was blocked and they thought the attackers came from there. I knew Movea was a townland inhabited mostly by Catholics who were staunch Hibernians entirely opposed to Sinn Féin.

Fearing that murders would be committed, I directed the driver to turn up the Movea Road when we came to it. The 'B' Head and his car also came up. When we got to the first house in Movea, I found a regular army of 'B' Specials. They had come up from Stewartstown and other districts miles away, proving that the whole thing was pre-arranged. Two of the Specials were coming out of the farmer's house as I arrived. I asked what they were doing in that house, and they shouted at me that they were searching for the men that had attacked them.

At this time they were all crowded round me and I saw that unless I acted firmly, outrages would be committed. I told them that I was in charge of the district and that no more searching was to be done, unless under my personal supervision. Also, they were not to enter a house unless requested by me to do so. If they had suspicion of any house, I would search it and they could send one of their own men along with me and 'B' Head McClelland. We would search any house they named, properly and legally.

They agreed, and the first house they named was a Widow Dillon's, so accompanied by the 'B' Head and a 'B' Constable, I knocked at Dillon's door. A voice inside asked, who was there, and I answered, police. The voice inside said, 'Our house was raided only a few nights ago by men who said they were police, and they took our shotgun. I don't think they were police at all.'[2] I told them I was the Head Constable from Cookstown, to which the voice replied, 'If it's you, Head, I'll open at once', and she did so.

In the house we found Mrs Dillon, a feeble old woman in bed, her daughter and two sons, Edward and Patrick. We searched the house and found nothing suspicious. In compliance with an order issued some time previously, I got Edward Dillon to sign a certificate stating that during the search no damage had been committed. I have the certificate here before me as I write. On leaving Dillon's, I asked the 'B' Special who accompanied us where the next house he wanted to search was, and he said Bloomers'. This house was only about 100 yards from Dillons'.

When I got there I found that, notwithstanding my order that no searching was to be done except by me and the 'B' Head, the other 'B' men had been in Bloomers' and had the two young boys, Francis and Robert Bloomer, out of the house in the yard and had them standing with their hands above their heads and guns against their chests. One of the Specials shouted, 'These fellows were not long in bed – look at their collars, they hadn't the time to take off their collars.'

I went up and examined their collars, first releasing them from their perilous position by ordering the guns away and telling them to put down their hands. The collars, I found, were attached to their shirts – sewn to their shirts. Knowing that country boys sleep in their day shirts at night, I said to the 'B' Head, 'These collars are attached to their shirts and they couldn't take off their collars without removing the shirts.' He agreed and I ordered the boys into the house. In the house we found their father, a poor, frightened, harmless man. After searching and finding nothing suspicious we left.

On getting outside, I told the assembled crowd of so-called Special police that as they had disobeyed my order by entering Bloomers' house when I was in Dillons', no more searching would be done that night. I ordered them to get into their cars and return to their homes and barracks. Luckily, they reluctantly obeyed me, some of them shouting that I should have arrested the Bloomers. I got into the Crossley, or rather into the front seat with the driver, and we started for Cookstown, the other cars following.

As soon as we started, these so-called police started to sing Dolly's Brae and Kick the Pope, at the same time firing volleys of bullets in the air. When we got to Cookstown some of the Tullyhogue

Specials who had come into the town asked me to send the Crossley car out with them. Fearing that they could return to Movea, I went out with them and returned to Cookstown sometime about 3 or 4 am on the 21 June 1921 in a wretched state of mind, but glad that, as far as I knew, there had been no person murdered.

It was not long, however, until another bogus attack was planned, and I confess that on this occasion, notwithstanding my previous experience of their rascally conduct, I was almost convinced that it was genuine. As with all criminals, they overlooked a very small item in the staging of the play which convicted them beyond a shadow of a doubt. It was on the 29 June 1921, only 9 days after the Annaghmore ambush, while the District Inspector was still on holidays.

At about 3 pm I was called to the telephone. It was the sergeant of Gortin barracks who was trying to speak, but through some cause he could not convey his message, but said he would wire. In about half an hour I got a wire saying Herbert McAdoo had been held up by armed and masked men near Cock of the North Hill, and his goods had been burnt and his car taken to H--- Lodge.[3]

McAdoo was a draper in Cookstown who used to hawk drapery up through the Tyrone mountains and sell his stuff amongst the poor Catholic farmers. He conveyed his stuff in a Ford car. There was no alternative for me, except to get ready and go to the scene, so I ordered the cars to prepare. I had only done this when the 'B' Head Constable Sidney McClelland walked into the office and said to me, 'Did you get a wire?' I said yes. He then said, 'I am after getting one at the same time', pulling the wire out of his pocket and showing it to me.

It was from McAdoo himself. I was relieved to learn that McAdoo was uninjured, because the wire said, 'Am returning, inform wife'. These were the last words of the wire. The first words were almost the same as the sergeant's wire to me. At the time, I had no doubt whatever that this was a genuine outrage, but I was at a loss to know why McAdoo wired to McClelland. Couldn't he, I thought, have wired his wife directly, or his assistants, or some neighbour? McClelland's house was half a mile distant from his. Before long, I was to learn without doubt the reason.

McClelland was to be the principal man in the 'play', and it was McAdoo's duty, after having performed his part, to make sure by wiring that I would not go without the principal actor. According to plan, McClelland then said to me, 'I suppose you are going out there'. I said 'Yes, I have ordered the cars to get ready'. He then said, 'I have four "good men" for you'.

Knowing that it would be an unpardonable offence to refuse the services of the 'B' [Specials] I said 'All right, they can have the Ford car, I'll take my own men in the Crossley'. Before I could get my own men out, McClelland was back with three 'B' men, so that he was one of the four 'good men' himself.

Not a man in the station knew where the place was but we knew it was in the mountains between Kildress and Gortin. While I was getting my party ready I told him [McClelland] to go on with the Ford and tell the Sergeant at Kildress to be ready with his men to join me in the Crossley as soon as I arrived. He did so, and when I arrived there Sergeant Lynham and his party joined us. We proceeded through Dunamore and by enquiring found our way over Cock of the North Hill and eventually came to H--- Lodge, where we found McAdoo's car without a scratch on it.

On finding the vehicle undamaged, I said to McClelland that it was well to find the car, but he said, 'It's not the car we want to find, but the fellows who took it'. I agreed that it would be well if we could, but that I thought it unlikely they would still be in the neighbourhood, as the alleged offence was committed at 11 am and it was then about 6 pm. It was a holiday, 29 June, and the country people were not working. I noticed, before going to the avenue where the car was, two old farmers in their shirt sleeves admiring the crops, and while I was speaking to the 'B' Head about finding the car, I chanced to look in their direction. I saw two of the Specials had the two farmers with their hands up and guns to their chests. I ran down and released them, one of them assuring me that they knew nothing of anything being done, and that if anything wrong had been done, neither they or anyone in that locality had anything to do with it.

I then interrogated the woman who lived inside the Lodge, but she knew nothing, only that some men left the car inside the gate. There is a mountain just behind the Lodge and on coming from speaking to the woman I saw nearly all the Specials running up the mountain. I asked the nearest one why they were running, and he said, 'There's two after jumping from behind that wall and running over the hill'. I did not believe him as I could see no trace of any such men. Fearing what the Specials might do if I let them over the hill out of my view, I sounded my whistle and signalled for them to come back.

They did so, and McClelland, having seen them returning, came up and asked me who brought them back. I said that I did, and that we should get the cars ready before it was dark, as there might be a real attack on us if we were out after dark. He then drew his revolver (being a Head Constable he was allowed to carry a revolver; sergeants and constables had to carry rifles), flourishing it round his head. He said, 'Let them come, I'm ready for them'.

I took no notice of his swaggering, but having got the party together and tied McAdoo's car to the back of the Crossley started to tow it home. The Ford car with McClelland and his Specials brought up the rear. It was then about 7 pm on this June evening, and we were returning at a nice pace of about 20 mph until we came to the Cock of the North Hill. It is a round base hill, or what we called in Monaghan a 'knowe' egg, or cone-shaped hill, and the road ran right over the top of it.

I was sitting on the front seat along with the driver (a Belfast ex-corner boy whose wife was continually writing to me about him not sending any money) on the Crossley car, which was leading. The Ford was about 50 yards behind the towed car, so that when I got to the top of the hill and began to descend to the other side, I was out of sight of those in the Ford. It was just at this moment that several shots rang out and the driver shouted with an oath, 'We are attacked'. I called on him to stop the car, and he did so in a few yards.

We were then at the bottom of the hill. I got off as quickly as I could and got behind a dry stone wall on the near side of the road and drew my revolver, the only time I ever drew it, or any other firearm, with the intention of defending myself. All the other men in the Crossley got out and lay on the other side of the road with their guns ready.

After I got across the wall, I noticed an old man and a girl within a few yards of me coming to the road from the other side pushing a water cart. Immediately two of the Specials made a rush at him with their guns. I shouted at them not to touch that old man and as there was no sign of the enemy, saw that the old man and the girl got away without being further molested.

At this time, one of the party, I could not say whether it was a 'B' or an 'A' [Special], shouted, 'They are away on the bog'. There was a bog, or low-lying ground, to the right, and without waiting for an order of any kind, more than half the party, including the 'B' Head and his men, went over the fence and rushed along the bog, shooting as they went. I ran up to those who remained and ordered them to stay with the cars.

It was then that the driver lifted two petrol bins out of the Crossley car, and throwing them on the grass on the side of the road near where I was standing, shouted; 'Look at my petrol bins bored'. I looked and there I saw what looked like real undoubted proof that an attack had been made on us. The petrol was running out of the tins through bullet holes. I asked where the tins had been and was told, in the car behind me. I told him to put the tins back into the car in the exact place they had been in when the shots were fired.

He did so, and I noticed that when the tins were upright there was no petrol escaping, the holes being above the level of the petrol in them. It was only when they were thrown on their side that petrol escaped. It then occurred to me that if the tins were bored by bullets fired at us going over the hill, there must be a corresponding hole, or holes, in the wooden sides of the car.

I examined minutely the box (all my Crossley tenders had a wooden box about two feet high, so that the petrol tins were surrounded by a wooden wall, as it were, and anything that would be thrown or fired at the car would have to go through this wood before it could touch the petrol tins, unless it was dropped from the air), but could find no corresponding hole in the box. That was the only item of a very elaborate program that they missed.

All the 'artistes', from McAdoo down to the driver, had acted their parts splendidly, but the driver, when making holes in the petrol tins before leaving Cookstown, either forgot or overlooked the necessity of making corresponding holes in the box of the Crossley, and as a result spoiled the whole performance.

As soon as I made this discovery, I told the driver to keep sounding the horn, and kept blowing my own whistle to get the party back who had ran after an imaginary enemy through the bog. In a short time two of them came into view, kicking an old man in front of them. As they were ill-treating him, I went towards them and found that it was the old man who was pushing the water cart when the alleged attack began.

I asked him if he was not the old man who was drawing the water. He replied that he was, and that they came into his house and took him out and kicked him. I sent him back and ordered them to their cars. In a short time the remainder returned. They had another prisoner with them who, I discovered, was a young Englishman who had only arrived in the locality a few days previously on a visit to his cousin, with whom he had been out walking.

On seeing the police running and shooting, he ran behind a fence for shelter from the bullets. I sent him home as well and got them all into the cars, but before continuing the journey home I told Sergeant Lynham of my discovery about the petrol tins and of my being sure there had been no attack. I also told him that I anticipated another attack before we would get home and directed him to keep a watch on the Ford car behind. It turned out that I was right in my anticipation.

When we were within a short distance of Dunamore Parochial Hall, as the Crossley car went round a sharp bend, out of view of the Ford, more shots rang out and the driver again shouted, 'Another attack, keep your heads down'. At the same time, a Special named Lewis who was in the Crossley behind where I was sitting, stood up and said, 'There's seven or eight men behind that hedge'. He pointed to a fence running at right angles to the road. I again told the driver to stop and called Lewis to come and show me the seven or eight men.

He and Swindall came running after me. As they were running, they collided and fell. A bullet from one of their rifles went off past me. I do not know whether it was accidental or otherwise, but when we got to the fence there were no men there, as I well knew, so I caught hold of Lewis and ordered him into the car. I told him I would put him into the lock-up when I got to Cookstown. While I was seeing him into the car, I noticed the others with their rifles pointing to a hill covered with furze behind the (Parochial) Hall.

In the midst of the furze there was an old man, a typical old Irishman with a high hat sitting taking the air. They were lying on the fence with their guns turned towards the poor old man. I shouted at them to put their rifles down and get into the car. They did so, and when I got back to the Ford car in which the 'B' Head and his three other 'good men' were, I told them that if there was another shot fired I would make prisoners of them all.

There was no more firing – the alleged enemy ceased fire at the same time as I gave orders to my own heroes. When we got to Kildress and stopped to leave off the Sergeant and his party, one of the Specials showed me where the butt of his rifle had been bored by a bullet. Another had the rim of his cap touched so that the whole of them had their part to play in the performance.

On returning to Cookstown, we delivered McAdoo's car to him. He had returned earlier in the evening, safe and sound after having successfully got through his part of the program. It was a successful day for him, and in addition to his having done his bit for the cause, he got well paid for his day's work. At least I believe he got compensation ... As for me, I do not think I ever spent a more miserable night. I knew as well as I was alive that the whole thing was bogus from start to finish, but how was I to prove it? The dice was loaded against me.[4]

Notes

1. This incident was reported in the *Newsletter* dated 21 June 1921, as follows:

Ambush Near Cookstown-Special Constables Attacked.

"B" Specials ambushed at Annagh at 1.a.m yesterday. The patrol took cover and returned the fire which appeared to come from across a field of corn. For upwards of an hour the firing continued, but without damage to anyone, and when reinforcements arrived from Cookstown the ambushers had disappeared.

Several cartridges were found, some of which had the nose sawn off and one was dum-dum. Two sticks of gelignite, with detonators, were also found. It is assumed that the party had been on the way to blow up a small bridge, and make the roads impassable. The road behind, leading to Pomeroy, was blocked with large bushes, apparently to prevent pursuit. No arrests have yet been made.

Although McKenna mentioned returning from the events of that night in the small hours of 21 June, and the *Newsletter* of that date referred to an attack on the previous day, which would make it 20 June, he may have got his dates slightly mixed up.

The *Tyrone Courier* dated Thursday 23 June 1921 described the same incident as follows:

SPECIALS AMBUSHED
ATTACKED NEAR SANDHOLES
Dum Dum Bullets and Gelignite Found

The first attack on the Special constables who patrol the roads in Cookstown district took place on Monday morning at Annagh, on the road to Sandholes, and about four miles from Cookstown.

The report went on to describe the supposed attack just before 1 am which apparently lasted for an hour, although the Tullylagan Specials suffered no casualties. The shooting was heard by the Specials on patrol in Cookstown, who immediately reported to the barracks, and the Head Constable ordered out the motors to proceed to the place with all the men available. The B men were called out, and in a few minutes four motors and a Crossley tender were filled, and just before leaving a motor cycle with one of the Tullylagan B Specials arrived and gave more precise information. When the contingent from Cookstown arrived at the scene they found upwards of 100 Specials at the place, fully armed. Search parties were organised and a number of houses were visited.

> The report described the subsequent search, with four 'live cartridges' found in the surrounding area, one of which was a

... dum-dum bullet. Later in the day another cartridge with the bullet slit was found at the same place. They had evidently been dropped in the hurried departure of the ambushers. Another very important find was made during the morning by Mr George McCartney, R.D.C.- two sticks of gelignite wrapped up in paper and with detonators. The explosives were handed to the District Commander of the "B" Specials.

> It may have been that the sticks of gelignite were later additions McKenna was unaware of at the time, or perhaps he just forget to mention them when writing his memoir eleven years later. It was remarkable that the supposed attack by the IRA ceased just as the reinforcements under Head Constable McKenna arrived from Cookstown. It seemed to be another case of the Unionist officer class of the RIC colluding with the Specials in order to make it appear there was a greater level of Republican activity than was actually the case. This echoed McKenna's earlier experiences in Carnlough, when he was expected to collude with his superiors in exaggerating the level of Ulster Volunteer activities in his area.
>
> Once again, McKenna's description of events in the memoir match the reports of the time as the *Tyrone Courier* mentioned the Head Constable (McKenna) taking out the Crossley. It did not mention that McKenna was acting District Inspector at the time, or that the patrol apparently attacked belonged to the same group of Specials involved in Joseph Hayden's killing (see McKenna's opening paragraph of this section on p. 73). It concluded the report by saying that:

On Friday night two men were seen at Grange putting up printed proclamations in the name of the I.R.A., and which stated that Catholics were being harassed and threatened; that if any outrage was committed on the person or property of Catholics who live in the district the perpetrators, "who are well known to the I.R.A., and the associates of the perpetrators in other districts will be summarily dealt with whenever, however, and wherever opportunity offers." - By order I.R.A.

> This gives the impression that the IRA were active in the rural hinterland of Cookstown, which is partially verified (see Cookstown section with mention of McDermott) by McKenna agreeing that a genuine 'Sinn Féin outrage' had happened at Dunamore when a postman was robbed.
>
> 2. The following report involves the same two families described here. Judging by the date used by McKenna, i.e. the early hours of 21 June 1921, the incident reported in this *Irish News* of Wednesday 29 June 1921 related to a different occasion. It refers to Sunday 26 June, five days after the incident in the memoir:

Cookstown Residents Maltreated

On Sunday morning the houses of Mr George Bloomer and Mrs Dillon, situate in the townlands of Moveagh and Gorteor, near Cookstown, were raided by armed and disguised men, who took out young Bloomer and threatened to shoot him if he would not tell where there were firearms.

They also took out Mrs Dillon's two sons, charging Eddie with having a gun, which had been seized by the Specials but afterwards returned. The young men were then taken to a lonely part of the road, tied together and beaten with the butts of rifles. It is believed that the persons who thus maltreated them were "B" Specials.

> It would appear that the Specials revisited the Bloomers and Dillons a matter of days later, presumably having on this occasion no RIC officer with them. This persistent harassment in the dead of night, particularly in the aftermath of the Hayden murder must have instilled fear among isolated nationalists in the rural hinterland of Cookstown.
>
> The personal injury claims of the Specials' victims were mentioned in the *Tyrone Courier* dated 25 August 1921:

Robert Bloomer, of Moveagh, claimed £200 for malicious injuries.

Patrick Dillon, of Gorticar, (Doris) claimed £200 for malicious injuries.

Edward Dillon, of Gorticar, (Doris) claimed £200 for malicious injuries.

Criminal Injuries records of the time show that Robert Bloomer of Moveagh was awarded £7 over the incident, for being maimed or maliciously injured on 26 June 1921 at Gorticar (Doris). The witness names were Dr James Gillespie, Edward Dillon and Patrick Dillon, with the latter two also recorded elsewhere as claimants.

The concern expressed in the letter from the RIC Divisional Commander to the RIC County Commander in Tyrone after the murder had not filtered through to operations on the ground. The Specials were still operating in the district unfettered by the presence of RIC officers.

3. This is how the location appears in the original memoir. It may be that McKenna had forgotten the full name 11 years later.

4. Herbert Nathaniel McAdoo made a Criminal Injuries claim for the incident, which occurred at Mennascalla and Kinigillen on 29 June 1921. The total claim included: a) the burning and destroying of draper goods and stock in trade, £300; b) damaging and injuring motor car, £60; c) expenses incurred in connection with malicious injury, £120; d) loss of business, £500. The overall claim was settled at £275, 'to be levied off the County at large.'

The *Tyrone Courier* edition of Thursday 7 July 1921 carried the following report:

COOKSTOWN MAN'S MOTOR SEIZED
Exciting Incidents in the Mountains

... Mr H.R. McAdoo, draper, Cookstown, was on business in a motor car delivering goods in the mountain district between Cookstown and Gortin last week, when, at Meenascallagh, about 10 miles from Cookstown, he was held up by armed and disguised men, who took his car and goods. The goods were burned on the roadside and the car removed, some of the party saying they were taking it to Formil, about 2 miles further into the mountains, where it would be burned.

Subsequently the Cookstown police found the motor at Formil which they took back with them. When they reached the district in which Mr McAdoo had been held up they were received with a volley of bullets from an ambushing party, and though no-one was struck all had narrow escapes.

The police dismounted and fired on the attacking party,

one man being seen to fall. The attackers retreated, and near the door of a house a bicycle was found, which no-one about that house would claim. After searching several houses in the sparsely populated district the party once more set off, and about a mile further down the road were again shot at, but as it was then quite dark they did not stop and got safely back to Cookstown.

> The details in the report differ greatly from McKenna's account, and perhaps give a clue as to how his superiors dressed up the incident as regards the apparent IRA attacks.
> Another report in the same edition of the *Courier*, referring to an event subsequent to the McAdoo incident, reads as follows:

SNIPERS IN COOKSTOWN AREA

Following the ambush at Meenascallagh, about ten miles from Cookstown, last week, when a party of police were twice fired at when out rescuing a motor car seized by Sinn Féiners and the contents burned, a thorough search of the district was organised by the police on Sunday morning. At an early hour in the morning a man named Monaghan ... came to a small group of police and said that he had been shot. On examination it was found that he had a bullet wound in the back of the neck, a bullet actually passing in and out through the flesh. He said that it came from the lower road, and as none of the search party were on the road, at the time it is presumed that the shot was fired by civilians, who were sniping the police all morning from the direction of Formil. During the search the police discovered a quantity of poteen in several houses.

> The *Irish News* of 3 July 1921 reported the same incident in a starkly different way, stating clearly that the men involved were all police and 'B' Specials:

John Monaghan, Bellivena Beg, aged 60 years, was returning to his house about 9 o'clock in the morning, when he saw some lorries stop about a quarter of a mile away. The men in them got out and broke up into batches of four or five. One of these batches came towards him and fired three or four shots, and he felt a sting in his neck and fell on his knees ... another section of the force came on the scene and searched him. They asked him for his pistol. He said he never had one in his life and that it was their comrades who had shot him.

The *Irish News* mentioned in the same report 'the burning of the beautiful parochial hall' and described:

> evidence of the use of bombs, the walls having been blown out in two places. The carrying of tins of petrol into the hall was seen. A neighbouring public house was raided at about 3.30 am. It is stated drink was ordered and not paid for. The house of Father O'Connor, curate of the parish, was also raided. A lock up shop owned by a man named McGurk was broken into and two overcoats and a quantity of tobacco, it is alleged, were missing after the visit.

All this seemed on the face of it much more serious than a mere search, as suggested by the *Tyrone Courier*. Other incidents mentioned include the house of a Mr Monaghan being raided, although it is unclear if this is the same Monaghan allegedly shot by the Specials later in the morning. Also, the 'house of a man named Loughran was burned to the ground.'

The following report from the *Dungannon Democrat* of Wednesday July 13 described the same incidents, all of which apparently flowed from what McKenna claimed in his memoir to be two bogus attacks in the wake of the alleged theft of McAdoo's car. This may have been the unfortunate sequel to the memoir which the Head Constable did not mention.

"SPECIALS" ACTIVITY IN TYRONE
CATHOLIC HOUSES RAIDED AND WRECKED
Questions in British Parliament

In the English House of Commons on Thursday week, Mr. DEVLIN [leader of the Irish Party in Northern Ireland], by private notice, asked the Chief Secretary whether his attention had been drawn to the events at Kildress, Co. Tyrone, on Sunday morning last; whether he was aware that in the early hours of that morning over 30 lorries and motor cars conveying police and "B" special constables from Cookstown and Dungannon drove into the parish ... and proceeded to raid and wreck Catholic houses ... and set fire to the Parochial Hall ... a local public house was raided at about

3.30 a.m ... other shops and houses were raided and everything thrown into disorder in the course of the raid, which lasted about six hours.

> Doubtless there were consequences for all concerned within Cookstown barracks, but the real repercussions were reserved for the residents of Kildress and the surrounding area.
> The report went on to detail the Specials visiting a house and forcing the older of two little girls to 'sign a document that no harm had been done', the girls' parents being out at devotions in their local church. Also mentioned was an 'old man retiring to his house about nine o'clock [who] was fired at by some of the police without warning and seriously wounded' and 'people returning from Dunamore Church [who] were wantonly fired at without warning.' Joe Devlin enquired of the Chief Secretary 'who was responsible for this raid, and whether he would take steps immediately to disband this force.'
> Mr T. W. Brown, Solicitor General for Ireland, responded that he had been advised:

that a party of Crown forces in four lorries and 14 motor cars visited Kildress on the date mentioned to search for arms owing to the police having been fired at in the locality. A public house and a number of shops and houses were searched, but the allegation that the public house was raided for drink was denied. An old man was slightly wounded ...

Mr. DEVLIN - In view of the universal acts of rowdyism and attacks on innocent people by these special constables- (cries of dissent) - who are not really constables at all, but only Volunteers from Ulster with the authority of the Crown behind them, will the right hon. Gentleman state what is being done to protect innocent Catholic citizens in Ulster towns?

Mr. BROWN - I do not know of any such state of affairs as the hon. Member refers to.

Mr DEVLIN - Will this House afford any protection to innocent people murdered in the dead of night by the forces of the Ulster Volunteers ...

No answer was given.

Conclusion

This final passage which continues the memoir is partly illegible. The dots indicate illegible words. It is clear that McKenna simply stopped writing after the words 'the affair ended'.

Before making a report next day I went out to Kildress to Sergeant Lynham to see if he would back up my statement if I said there were no shots fired at us. He could not or would not (next 50 words or so illegible) ... Further, I believe ... my own officer ... before he went on leave ... so I could see a loophole for me [to] escape reporting the alleged outrage in the usual way, so I made a report saying about the receipt of the wire and about our going there and finding the car, casually mentioning that on our return home shots were fired ... but that we ... no person was injured. It would not have been too bad had the affair ended ...

END OF MEMOIR

The text ends here, petering out with McKenna halting his narrative. It is difficult now to imagine what the repercussions were for McKenna of the allegedly faked attack. Within a few months he had left Cookstown for Kildare, where he would be disbanded the following year.

As McKenna acknowledged, it would be difficult for him to prove his version of events. Naturally, the passing of the years since then has made this impossible today, both where the McAdoo incident and others were concerned. He may have found himself unable or unwilling to point out the bogus nature of the attack by referring to the wooden surround in the police lorry being unmarked by bullets. He had been put in a difficult position, as he would have had to prove that a group of Specials were conspiring against him.

As with history, so with the memoir – much depends on what facts are chosen and how they are interpreted by the person recording them. But there is no doubt that the Co. Tyrone described in the memoir contained in microcosm the problems which had already, and would in the future, beset Northern Ireland. The belief of the Nationalist majority in Tyrone that they would form part of the Free State was reflected in T.J.S. Harbinson's (MP for North East Tyrone) warning to Lloyd George in 1920

> that the coercion of Tyrone into what is called ... Ulster will be one of the most difficult propositions that any government has yet set before it.

Harbinson did not realise the extent to which the British Government would give the Unionists carte blanche to establish their authority over the six counties, including Tyrone and Fermanagh where they formed a minority. Like many Nationalists, he believed the British Government would not coerce counties into the new Northern Ireland state against the will of a majority of its people.

John McKenna's memoir shows how he perceived his time in the RIC. His memories are those of an ordinary Catholic policeman who lived in difficult times, devoutly religious but dedicated to the impartial administration of the law under British rule. It could be argued that his placing any faith in the law he upheld was mistaken, that his brand of moderate Redmondite Nationalism was doomed from the start as far as the north being included within the Home Rule Act was concerned. Yet the Sinn Féin variety of Nationalism also failed the northern minority, as the coercion of a million unionists into the Irish Free State was always going to be a non-starter.

The siege mentality of both Ulster Loyalists (in the context of the entire island of Ireland) and Ulster Nationalists (in the context of north east Ireland) over the period covered in the memoir meant that an agreed solution was always going to be problematic. Yet the British government's lack of foresight in dividing Ulster to guarantee a Unionist majority without any minority safeguards may have been primarily responsible for the protracted problems of the next eighty years.

A nine county Ulster state under direct rule or a devolved parliament may have had the potential for a peaceful resolution of Ireland's problems. Yet that was never going to be a viable proposition for the Unionists, whose primary objective was to ensure that Ulster or a substantial part of it remained within the United Kingdom. Adhering to the historic nine county province may have presented them with a temporary or unstable local majority.

The 'B' Specials are now reviled in the Catholic folk memory, whereas some Loyalists still see their historic role as providing a bulwark against a Dublin parliament. That the political and religious identity of their opponents was then synonymous in the eyes of many Loyalists may have been inevitable, given the close identification of Catholic Nationalists and [to an extent] Republicans with their Church. Yet for ordinary Catholics on the ground, such as McKenna, who held no brief for the violence of Republicans, the assumption that all Catholics supported violence was outrageous and led to serious injustices.

McKenna's posting to Cookstown in November 1920 may have appeared to him at the time as a good move, as his family still lived in Larne. Yet he came there only four months after an IRA attack on Cookstown Barracks, which led to the death of the first IRA man to die in the northern campaign at that time. The attack took place on 18 June 1920.

Richard Abbott, in *Police Casualties in Ireland, 1919–22*, describes the attack:

> Conway and three other Constables from the west of Ireland, all with Sinn Féin sympathies, were stationed in Cookstown. One of them, Denis A. Leonard, who had

been reduced from the rank of Sergeant because of his sympathies, contacted a prominent Sinn Féin man in Cookstown at the end of March 1920 to discuss their proposal for the IRA to take over Cookstown Barracks. A few weeks later Conway and Leonard, with two IRA officers from Dungannon, attended a meeting in Keady, Co. Armagh, at which it was decided to carry out a raid on the Cookstown Barracks on 4 June 1920. However, this attack did not take place as the IRA men from Keady and Dungannon who were to participate in it feared that they might walk into a carefully prepared trap, as their scouts reported unfavourably on the proposed attack, believing the Barracks had been taken over by the military.

The four Constables again made contact with the IRA and succeeded in getting the raid rescheduled for 17 June 1920. However, two of the Constables, one being Conway, were sent on temporary duty to other Barracks in the area. The IRA were informed of this but intimated that they would continue with the plan. So on the agreed date IRA men from Dungannon and Keady entered the Barracks via an unlocked back door, but when two of their number tried to enter a locked bedroom belonging to Head Constable Henry O'Neill shots were exchanged which awakened the remaining sleeping policemen and a great deal of shooting followed in which one of the IRA men was seriously wounded.

Constable Leonard was dismissed from the RIC after the raid, with Constables Conway, Hagarden and O'Boyle resigning within the following three months. Abbott states that Conway later joined the IRA in Fermanagh. For all that, the raid was a one-off, and did not appear to have much input from Cookstown civilians. It does help us understand the Unionist attitude towards the RIC at the time, as the Constabulary was thought to be full of southern Catholics who were not to be trusted. In this case at least, their suspicions were well grounded.

The constables mentioned were, as McKenna was, Irish Nationalists. They choose to express this differently. Constable Hagarden and his associates' time in Cookstown Barracks proved uncomfortable from the outset, as shown in the *Memoirs of Constable Jeremiah Mee, RIC*:

> Most of their comrades were North of Ireland Protestants and Loyalists. As a result of numerous heated discussions in the barracks mess room on the political situation at that time a serious antagonism developed between these four men and the rest of the garrison ... eventually, because of some vicious baiting of Constable Denis Leonard – whose Sinn Féin sympathies were notorious and for which he had been reduced in rank from sergeant to constable in 1915 – the four decided at the end of March 1920 to facilitate an IRA raid on Cookstown police barracks ...

The incident, when it eventually occurred in June 1920, was reported in the *Irish Independent* of 18 June, as follows:

Constables Hagarden and Henderson who were on guard were at once overpowered, disarmed and tied up. The raiders, who had taken off their boots, then went upstairs, according to the *Belfast Telegraph*, to the room where the eleven year old daughter of Head Constable Henry O'Neill was sleeping. They carried her down to the guardroom and, in answer to her pathetic appeals not to shoot her father or mother, they assured her that no harm would come to her or her parents.

Meanwhile other raiders knocked at the Head Constable's bedroom door and, in answer to his enquiry as to who was there, the reply came, 'officer', in tones which were an almost perfect imitation of District Inspector George Hall's voice. Two shots were then fired through the door, one bullet passing within a few inches of the Head Constable's head. He immediately returned the fire with his revolver and the raiders retired from the barracks.

The other members of the garrison were then aroused, their comrades released, and the defence began. Bullets rained on the back of the barracks, on which side the greater portion of the attacking force was concentrated. Bombs and hand grenades were used freely on both sides ...

After the raiders had withdrawn the police found blood-stained handkerchiefs and traces of blood in the vicinity. They also found several pairs of boots and stockings. It was

found that the wires to Dungannon had been cut while it is stated an attempt had been made to deplete the Cookstown garrison by rumours of a contemplated attack on Coagh police barracks the same night, as a result of which a sergeant and two constables were sent to Coagh that same evening ...
District Inspector Hall, who does not reside in the barracks, was awakened by the firing and made his way to assist the garrison.
When word of the attack reached Dungannon early yesterday morning, police at once set out in motor cars for Cookstown. On nearing Newmills they met a motor car, which they stopped, and found it contained Patrick Loughran, Quinn's Lane, Dungannon, who was in a state of collapse.

The IRA raid was organised by Republicans from Dungannon, presumably because there were no active IRA men in Cookstown. But the involvement of RIC men with the IRA may shed some light on the attitude of some of McKenna's colleagues towards him when he took charge of the Cookstown Barracks only a matter of months later. This real attack, assisted by IRA sympathisers within the barracks, would have given the Specials and others another reason for equating Catholic RIC men with Republicanism.

In his book entitled *The 'B' Specials – A history of the Ulster Special Constabulary*, Sir Arthur Hezlet points out that many Specials believed that many RIC officers had Sinn Féin sympathies, and routinely took part in operations which did not involve consulting the force at all. It was only a short step for such people to associate all Catholic RIC men with violent Republicanism and the Church Triumphant, with all the attendant fears and prejudices.

McKenna himself was aware that not all Specials or Black and Tans were as prejudiced as they were reputed to be, as he considered Swindall the Special and Wilson the Black and Tan to be 'decent' men.

This was the then recent history of the Cookstown RIC barracks to which McKenna was posted in charge of in November 1920. The Specials did not always distinguish between law-abiding Catholics and those who had broken the law, whether inside or outside the RIC. McKenna fell into the law-abiding category, as did many civilian victims of the Specials in the Cookstown district during the period of the memoir.

History shows that Northern Ireland itself was predestined to fall into a similar trap. It would treat Catholics with suspicion and as potential, if not actual, collaborators with Irish Republicanism. This represented a failure by the ruling class and their supporters to distinguish between different political viewpoints within the Catholic community. It led to the estrangement of Catholics who would otherwise have been amenable to the concept of Home Rule within the British Empire, as espoused by John Redmond, and supported by the likes of John McKenna – and many others. It also meant that co-operation with Unionism would be made more difficult.

The disturbances surrounding the Eucharistic Congress in 1932 confirmed for McKenna what he had suspected since the creation of the new Northern Irish state in 1921 – the Catholicism he held dear had almost been equated with treasonable activity. Out of this realisation came McKenna's polemical memoir in the aftermath of the 1932 Congress. The events in his career, particularly those which occurred in Northern Ireland, inevitably led to the feeling that his RIC career may have futile. He represented those Catholic Irishmen who simultaneously considered themselves both British citizens and Irish nationalists.

Home Rule might have worked for Ireland as a whole, as McKenna hoped, but its success depended on the two communities in Ireland trusting each other and agreeing to disagree on how they practised their religion and traditions. 'Live and let live' was not much in vogue in early-twentieth century Ireland, though happily it is at the core of the new institutions established under the Good Friday Agreement of 1998. In the early-twenty first century Northern Ireland faces the future with more optimism than it did one hundred years previously.

A Sequence of Historical Events

RELEVANT TO JOHN McKENNA'S LIFE

1891
02 March – John McKenna appointed as Constable in RIC.
October – Parnell, leader of the Irish Party, dies.

1892
23 January – John McKenna is allocated to Galway (West Riding). Gladstone, returned to power, introduces the Second Home Rule Bill, which is thrown out by the House of Lords.

1893
The Gaelic League is founded.

1895
The Tories return to power under Lord Salisbury.

1900
The Irish Party reunites under John Redmond.

1903
10 October – John McKenna is transferred to Antrim, his first posting in that district being to Ballymena.

1905
Arthur Griffith founds Sinn Féin.

1906
The Liberal Party is returned to power.
In November McKenna passes the 'P' exam in Dublin. He is placed 19th out of 100.

1907

June – McKenna is promoted to Sergeant, and in the same year obtains the Board of Trade Certificate as Inspector of Weights and Measures.

1908

08 April – Asquith is appointed Prime Minister. In this year McKenna is sent to take charge at the barracks in Carnlough, Co. Antrim.

1910

21 February – Edward Carson is made leader of the Ulster Unionist Party.

1911

23 September – Carson addresses a rally of Orangemen and Unionist Clubs at Craigavon, the Belfast residence of James Craig.

1912

11 April – Third Home Rule Bill introduced in the House of Commons.

02 May – motion proposing the exclusion of four Ulster counties from Home Rule defeated.

28 September – thousands sign the Ulster Solemn League and Covenant.

1913

01 January – Carson's amendment proposing the exclusion of Ulster from Home Rule defeated. The Home Rule Bill passed in the Commons on 16 January, but defeated in the Lords on 30 January. This happens again in July.

31 January – the Ulster Volunteer Force is formed. This in turn leads to the formation of the Irish Volunteers.

04 December – a royal proclamation forbids the importation of arms and ammunition into Ireland.

1914

16 April – McKenna makes his report that there are no Ulster Volunteers or Ulster Clubs in the Carnlough area.

24–5 April – the UVF runs guns into Larne.

25 May – an amended Home Rule Bill is passed in the Commons.

A government of Ireland Bill is introduced permitting the temporary exclusion of Ulster from Home Rule on a county by county basis. On 08 July the Lords alter the Bill to provide for Ulster's permanent exclusion.

29 June – McKenna is posted to Larne against his own wishes and contrary to the RIC's code of practice.

11 July – McKenna witnesses some of the weapons from the gun-running being stored in Larne Orange Hall, just across the road from the police barracks.

12 July – armed Ulster Volunteers parade through Larne and drill in the market place.

04 August – the United Kingdom declares war on Germany, and on 15 September the implementation of Home Rule is suspended for the duration of the War.

1915

25 May – a Coalition Government is formed, and Carson is appointed Attorney General.

1916

24 April – the Easter Rising begins in Dublin, ending on 29 April. By 23 May Lloyd George is put in charge of Irish-British negotiations, and by 07 December he succeeds Asquith as PM.

1918

06 March – John Redmond, leader of the Irish Party, dies.

18 April – the Catholic Church lends its support to the Anti-Conscription campaign spearheaded by Sinn Féin – conscription subsequently dropped by the government.

02 November – Lloyd George declares that he will introduce partition as part of any Home Rule Bill. By 11 November the War has ended.

December – the Irish Party is virtually obliterated by Sinn Féin in the General Election.

1919

21 January – Dáil Éireann meets and declares an Irish Republic. On the same day, the Anglo-Irish War begins with the killing of two RIC men by Irish Volunteers at Soloheadbeg, Co. Tipperary.

1920

02 January – the Black and Tans are formed, with the RIC Auxiliaries formed on 27 July.

11 September – Sergeant John McKenna is promoted to Head Constable and is posted to Kenmare, Co. Kerry.

01 November – Head Constable John McKenna is transferred to Cookstown in Co. Tyrone. In this month the Ulster Special Constabulary is launched.

23 December – the Government of Ireland Act, providing for partition, becomes law.

1921

4 February – James Craig succeeds Carson as Ulster Unionist leader.

19 May – Joseph Hayden, a Catholic farmer, is killed by 'B' Specials near Pomeroy, Co. Tyrone during a night raid unsupervised by RIC regulars. McKenna's superiors overrule his attempts to investigate.

24 May – elections to the Belfast and Dublin Parliaments take place.

June – McKenna is drawn into what he considers to be bogus attacks launched by the Specials in the Cookstown area. He believes his life is at risk. On the 07 June James Craig becomes Prime Minister of Northern Ireland, with the King opening Parliament on 22 June. Partition is established.

11 July – truce arranged between Irish and British forces in the Anglo-Irish War. The truce applies to all Ireland.

12 July – McKenna cannot use guns under the terms of the truce to combat the civil disturbances in Cookstown.

01 August – McKenna is posted to Co. Kildare ahead of the disbandment of the RIC in 1922.

11 October to 06 December – the Anglo-Irish treaty negotiations are held in London.

13 November – Griffith agrees to Lloyd George's suggestion of a Boundary Commission to determine the new border between Northern Ireland and the new Irish Free State.

22 November – the Northern Ireland Government takes over responsibility for law and order from the RIC in the six counties.

06 December – the Irish plenipotentiaries, led by Griffith and Michael Collins sign the Treaty, setting up a 26-county Free State with a

Boundary Commission to determine the final border between north and south.

1922
- 21 January – first Craig-Collins pact signed in London.
- 23 March – murder of McMahon family in Belfast by 'uniformed men'.
- 31 March – pact signed by Collins, Craig and representatives of the Irish Free State, Northern Ireland and British Governments.
- 22 May – murder of a Unionist MP, W.J. Twaddell, in central Belfast as sectarian violence escalates.
- 31 May – Royal Ulster Constabulary replaces RIC.
- 28 June – outbreak of Irish Civil War.
- 22 August – Collins shot dead in ambush at Béal na mBláth.
- 07 December – Northern Ireland opts out of the Irish Free State by a petition by its parliament to the King.

1925
- 3 December – collapse of Boundary Commission. The three governments sign the Tripartite Agreement, confirming the 1920 border.

1932
- 9 March – Eamon de Valera returned to power at head of a Fianna Fáil administration.
- 22–6 June 1932 – Eucharistic Congress held in Dublin – sectarian attacks on northern pilgrims.
- 2 October – Outdoor Relief riots in Belfast.

1935
July – eleven die in sectarian violence in Belfast – British troops deployed.

1939
3 September – outbreak of Second World War.

1943
Death of John McKenna, aged 72.

Bibliography

PUBLICATIONS

Richard Abbott, *Police Casualties in Ireland, 1919–22* (Mercier Press, Dublin, 2000).

Paul Bew, *Ideology and the Irish Question: Ulster Unionism and Irish Nationalism 1912–1916*, (OUP, Oxford, 1994).

John Brewer, *The RIC – An Oral History*, (Institute of Irish Studies, QUB, 1990).

Patrick Buckland *The Factory of Grievances: Devolved Government in Northern Ireland 1921–39*, (Gill & Macmillan, Dublin, 1979).

J. Anthony Gaughan, *Memoirs of Constable Jeremiah Mee, RIC*, (Anvil Books, Dublin, 1975).

Hansard 3, cccxlvi, 1149–50, 08 July 1890.

Sir Arthur Hezlet, *The 'B' Specials–A history of the Ulster Special Constabulary* (Mourne River Press, Belfast 1997).

Michael Laffan, *The Partition of Ireland, 1911–1925* (Dundalgan Press, Dundalk, 1983).

Geoffrey Lewis, *Carson, the Man Who Divided Ireland* (Hambledon Continuum, London, 2005).

Robert Lynch, *The Northern IRA and the Early Years of Partition, 1920–22*, (Irish Academic Press, Dublin, 2006).

Éamon Phoenix, *Northern Nationalism: Nationalist Politics, Partition and the Catholic minority in Northern Ireland 1890–1940*, (Ulster Historical Foundation, Belfast, 1994).

Thirty First International Eucharistic Congress Dublin, 1932, (Veritas, Dublin 1932).

MANUSCRIPTS AND DOCUMENTARY SOURCES

Edward O'Toole's recollection of the 1932 Eucharistic Congress, deposited in the National Archives, Dublin. This was written in the 1970's and deposited in the Archives in August 1978 [999/199/2].

Criminal Injuries Compensation Casebook for Co. Tyrone, 1921–2; PRONI (no reference number).
PRONI File HA8/494 – The Eucharistic Congress 1932.
PRONI File HA/5/161 'Relating to the proposed prosecution of 'B' Specials for the Murder of Joseph Hayden, Co. Tyrone.' Ministry of Home Affairs 'H' general files, 1921–2.
The 1911 Census, National Archives, Dublin.

NEWSPAPERS
Belfast Telegraph 14 May 1921 and 27 June 1932
Dungannon Democrat 13 July, 29 July 1921
Irish Independent, 18 June 1920
Irish News, 27 April 1914, 20 May, 29 June, 5 July, 14 July, 10 September 1921. Also reports regarding the Eucharistic Congress, June to August 1932
Irish Times 14 July 1921, 27 June 1932
Larne Times and Weekly Telegraph 2 May 1914 and 2 July 1932
Newsletter, 25 April 1914, 20 May, 21 June, 13 July, 14 July 1921
Tyrone Constitution, 15 July 1921
Tyrone Courier, 26 May, 16 June, 23 June, 14 July and 25 August 1921
Ulster Herald 28 May and 16 July 1921

Index

'A' Specials 40–41, 80
Abbott, Richard 92–93, 102
Agnew Street, Larne 10
Ancient Order of Hibernians xiii, 28, 34, 53, 75
Anglo-Irish Treaty, 1921 xvi, xvii, 70, 100–01
Anglo-Irish War, 1919–21 xv, xii, xiii, xvi, xviii, 30–32, 35, 99, 100
Annagap, Co. Monaghan xxi
Annagh, Co. Tyrone 83
Annaghmore, Co. Tyrone 73–74, 77
Anthony Essex 36
Antrim, County xii, xxvi, 12, 17, 18, 19, 22, 25, 26, 34, 97
Antrim, Glens of xiv, 2
Ardrahan, Co. Galway xx
Argenta 62
Armagh, County 34
Asquith, Herbert Henry xiv, 16, 21, 26, 35, 98, 99
Auxiliaries xv, 100

'B' Specials xvi–xvii, xix, 5, 12, 13, 32, 92, 95, 100
  and murder of Joseph Hayden xvi–xvii, 37, 55–72, 73, 84, 85, 100, 103
  in east Tyrone xvii, 37–45, 52–53, 54, 55–72, 73–89, 90–91, 95–96
  in Larne, 5, 12, 13
Balfour, Arthur James 31, 35
Ballinderry Bridge, Co. Tyrone 38, 53
Ballymena, Co. Antrim xiv, xxiii–xxv, 10, 17, 18, 19, 97
  See also Cullybackey Road, Ballymena
Balmoral, Belfast 34
Bamford, Charles 20
Banbridge, Co. Down 35
Bangor, Co. Down 23
Barna, Co. Galway xxiii
Barrington, District Inspector 2, 5

Bates, Sir Dawson 4, 9, 38, 39
Béal na mBláth, Co. Cork 101
Beck, Thomas 45
Belfast xiii, 1, 2, 10, 23, 26, 69, 70, 71, 79, 98, 100, 101, 103
  See also Balmoral, Belfast
    Craigavon, Belfast
    Musgrave Channel, Belfast
    Shankill Road, Belfast
    Stormont, Belfast
    Stranmillis University College, Belfast
Belfast Telegraph 13, 63, 94
Bellivena Beg, Co. Tyrone 87
Belloc, Hilaire 7
Bew, Paul 22, 102
Birrell, Augustine 22
Black and Tans xv, xvi, 32, 37, 44, 55, 95, 100
Bloomer, Francis 76
Bloomer, George 85
Bloomer, Robert 76, 85, 86
Boyne, Battle of the, 1690 53
Brewer, John 36, 102
Brooke, Sir Basil 71
Brown, T.W. 89
Buckland, Patrick 54, 102
Byrne, James xxi, xxiii, xxv
Byrne, Laurence xxi–xxii, xxiii, xxiv, xxv
Byrne, Mary xxiv, xxv
Byrne, Mazie xx
Byrne, Sarah xxi, xxii, xxiii, xxiv, xxv

Canavan, Hugh 48
Carnlough, Co. Antrim xiv, xxv, 4, 16, 17, 19–21, 22, 23, 25, 84, 98
Carrickfergus, Co. Antrim 2
Carson, Edward xv, 26, 34, 35, 37, 98, 99, 100, 102
Castledawson, Co. Derry 34
Cavan, County 22

Civil Service Commission 18
Claggan, Co. Tyrone 63, 65
Clyde Valley see *Mountjoy*
Coagh, Co. Tyrone 95
Cock of the North Hill, Co. Tyrone 77, 78, 79
Collins, Michael xvii, 100, 101
Conservative Party 35, 97
Conway, Constable 92–93
Cookstown, Co. Tyrone xvi, xvii, xxi, xxv, xxvi, 27, 33, 36, 37, 39–40, 41, 43–72, 74–77, 81, 82, 83, 84, 85, 86, 87, 88–89, 90, 92–93, 94, 95–96, 100
  See also Loy, Cookstown
   Oldtown Street, Cookstown
   Orritor Street, Cookstown
Cork, Co. Cork 16, 21
Cosgrave, W.T. 32, 36
Cosgrove, James 48, 49
Craig, Sir James xv, xvii, 70, 71, 98, 100, 101
Craigavon, Belfast 98
Creighton, Albert 50
Cromwell, Oliver 7
Crossdernott, Co. Tyrone 69
Cullybackey Road, Ballymena 11
Curragh, the, Co. Kildare xxv
Curran Road, Larne 9
Cushendall, Co. Antrim 20, 28

Daly, John 63, 65
Darragh, Robert 49
Darragh, William 48
de Valera, Eamon xvii, 13, 61–62, 101
Derry (City), Co. Derry 34, 43, 57, 59, 65, 66, 69
Derry, County 34
Devlin, Joe 34, 51, 88, 89
Devlin, Mr 51, 52
Devlin, William 57, 65, 66, 67, 68, 69
Dillon, Edward 76, 85, 86
Dillon, Mrs 75–76, 85
Dillon, Patrick 76, 85, 86
Donaghadee, Co. Down 23
Donnelly, Annie 48
Donnelly, Francis 10, 11
Dougherty, Sir James Brown 22
Down, County 34
Doyle, Mrs 47

Drumalis, Larne 24
Drumballyhue, Co. Tyrone 66
Drummond, Thomas xii
Dublin xii, xxv, xxx, 1, 2, 7, 9, 10, 12, 13, 14, 18, 25, 27, 30, 34, 35, 56, 69, 70, 92, 97, 99, 100, 101, 102, 103
  See also Kingsbridge, Dublin
   Phoenix Park, Dublin
Dublin Castle xii, xiii, 22, 45
Dublin Metropolitan Police 30
Dunamore Church, Co. Tyrone 89
Dunamore, Co. Tyrone 42, 78, 81, 85, 89
Dungannon Democrat 52, 88–89, 103
Dungannon, Co. Tyrone xvii, 40, 51, 56, 88, 93, 95
Dunlop, James 20–21
Dunne, William 36, 43

Easter Rising, 1916 xiii, xiv–xv, 27, 30, 34, 99
Eastwood, Henry Boyd 49
Eastwood, James 49
Eastwood, Thomas Joseph 49
Eastwood, William Francis 49
Eaves, Lieutenant-Colonel 66
Edwards, Sergeant Joseph 22
England xxv, 64
Ennisfeirt, Co. Kerry 36
Erwin, Francis 11
Eucharistic Congress, 1932 xii, xxv–xxvi, xxix–14, 32, 53, 96, 101, 102, 103

Falls, Edward, JP 66
Fanny 23
Farrell, M. xix
Fenians xii, xx
Fermanagh, County 34, 91, 93
Fianna Fáil 101
First World War xxi, 6, 25, 26, 27, 28, 34, 35, 99
Fleming, W.J. 47
Formil, Co. Tyrone 86, 87

Gaelic League 36, 97
Gallagher, Sergeant 45, 55–56, 74
Galway, County xx, xxi, xxiii, xxiv, xxv, xxvi, 17, 18, 53, 97

Gaughan, J. Anthony 102
George V, King 101
Germany 25, 26, 34, 35, 99
Getty, Mr 1
Giant's Causeway, Co. Antrim xxiv
Gillen, Charles 46, 49
Gillespie, Dr James xvii, 61–62, 63, 86
Gladstone, William 97
Glenarm, Co. Antrim 9, 36
Good Friday Agreement, 1998 96
Gort, Co. Galway xx
Gortavale, Co. Tyrone 65, 69
Gorteor, Co. Tyrone 85
Gortfad, Co. Tyrone 60, 62, 65, 68, 69
Gorticar, Co. Tyrone 85, 86
Gortin, Co. Tyrone 77, 78, 86
Grange, Co. Tyrone 84
Griffith, Arthur 97, 100

Hagan, Joseph 48
Hagan, Mr 43
Hagarden, Constable 93, 94
Hall, District Inspector George 38, 39–40, 41, 42–43, 44, 45, 48–49, 51, 53, 54, 55–58, 59, 61, 63, 67, 75, 77, 94, 95
Hamilton, Captain Andrew 13
Harbinson, Mr 52
Harbison, T.J.S. 61, 64, 91
Hayden, Dominic 62, 66, 68
Hayden, James 55–64, 66–71
Hayden, Joseph xvi–xvii, 53, 55, 57–72, 73, 84, 85, 100, 103
Hayden, Margaret 69
Hayden, Thomas 65, 68
Henderson, Constable 94
Henderson, Mr 39
Hezlet, Sir Arthur 53, 95, 102
Homburg, Germany 35
Home Rule xiii, xiv, xviii, xx, 8, 16, 19, 21, 22, 25, 26, 27, 32, 34, 35, 91, 96, 97, 98–99
Howth gun running, 1914 xiv, 27, 35
Hoy, J. 56, 64–65
Humphrey, Samuel 47, 49
Hunt, District Inspector 28–30, 35, 36
Hutchinson, Mr 66

Irish Civil War, 1922–23 101
Irish Constabulary xii
Irish Independent 94–95, 103
Irish League 20
Irish News 4, 7, 8–9, 10, 12–13, 22–23, 26, 34, 46–49, 53, 60–61, 63–64, 68, 71, 85, 87–88, 103
Irish Parliamentary Party *see* Irish Party
Irish Party 32, 34, 52, 88, 97, 99
Irish Republican Army xiii, xv, xviii, xxvi, 35, 36, 50, 53–54, 84–85, 87, 92, 93, 94–95, 102
Irish Republican Brotherhood xiii
Irish Times 13–14, 51, 103
Irish Volunteers xiii, xv, 36, 98

Jenkins, Mr 11
Jones, Thomas xix
Jordan, Duncan 66
Jordan, William 66

Keady, Co. Armagh 93
Kearney, James 48
Kelly, Father 3, 9, 10, 12, 13
Kenmare, Co. Kerry xvi, xxv, 33, 36, 100
Kerry, County xvi, 25, 26, 32, 36
Kettrick junction, Co. Kerry 36
Kildare, County xxv, 32, 90, 100
Kildress, Co. Tyrone 43, 44, 78, 82, 88–89, 90
Killarney, Co. Kerry 36
Kilrea, Co. Derry 53
Kingsbridge, Dublin 30
Kinigillen, Co. Tyrone 86

Laffan, Michael xix, 102
Land War xiii
Lappin, Mrs 48
Larne gun running, 1914 xiv, 14, 22–24, 27
Larne Times and Weekly Telegraph 10–11, 23–24, 103
Larne Urban Council 11–12
Larne, Co. Antrim xii, xiv, xviii, xxv, xxvi, xxvii, xxx, 1–6, 7–14, 16, 19, 21, 22, 23–25, 26–28, 33, 36, 44, 53, 92, 98, 99

See also Agnew Street, Larne
  Curran Road, Larne
  Drumalis, Larne
  McKenna Memorial School, Larne
  Old Glenarm Road, Larne
  St Joseph's Primary, Larne
  St MacNissi, Church of, Larne
Leonard, Constable Denis A. 92–93, 94
Lewis, Constable 81–82
Lewis, Geoffrey 35, 102
Liberal Party xiv, 22, 97
Lisburn, Co. Antrim 28
Lloyd George, David xv, 34, 91, 99, 100
London xxvi, xxvii, 32, 100
London, Midland and Scottish Railway 1, 4, 11
Londonderry, Lady 35
Lopdell, County Inspector 17
Loughran, Mr 88
Loughran, Patrick 95
Loughrey, John 3, 10
Lowis, Colonel 56
Loy, Cookstown 54
Lynch, Robert 53, 102
Lynham, Sergeant 44, 78, 81, 90

Mackin, Rev. J. 72
MacNeill, Eoin 32, 36
MacSwiney, Miss 31
Mageean, Bishop 4, 8–9
Maghera, Co. Derry 34
Magherafelt, Co. Derry 40, 42
Martin, District Inspector 12, 13
McAdoo, Herbert Nathaniel 73, 77–78, 79, 81, 82, 86, 87, 88, 90
McAnespie/McAnespy, Henry 48, 49
McCann, Mary Jane 48
McCartney, George 84
McClelland, Sidney ('B' Head Constable) 40, 41, 75–76, 77–78, 79, 80, 82
McClintock, Colonel 56–58
McConnell, Mr 11
McCullagh, Margaret 49
McCullough, Miss 48
McDermott, John 42–43, 85
McDonald, Sarah 48, 49
McDowell, R.B. xix
McErlean, Eileen 11
McGahan, John 48, 49

McGuigan, Father xxx, 1
McGurk, Mr 88
McGurkin, James 50, 51
McKenna Memorial School, Larne 2, 6, 10
McKenna, Mr (John's father) xxiii
McKenna, Father Francis 6
McKenna, Florence xxi, xxiv
McKenna, Henry Peter *see* McKenna, Peter
McKenna, James xxi, xxiv, 6
McKenna, Head Constable John 49, 51, 63, 84
McKenna, Katie xx, xxi–xxv, xxvi, 26
McKenna, Mary Jo xxiv
McKenna, Pauline xxi
McKenna, Peter xxi, xxiv, xxvii
McKenna, Rose xxi
McKenna, Tony xxi, xxvi
McKeown, Miss 48
McLaughlin, Rev. J. 50
McLaverty, Father Bernard 2, 3, 6–7, 8–9, 10, 12, 13
McMahon family 101
McMinn, Hugh 65, 66, 68, 69
McMinn, Jeremiah 66, 68, 69
Meath, County 28
Mee, Constable Jeremiah 94, 102
Meenascallagh, Co. Tyrone 86, 87
Mennascalla, Co. Tyrone *see* Meenascallagh, Co. Tyrone
Middlemas, K. xix
Monaghan, County xiii, xx, xxiii, 59, 79
Monaghan, John 87, 88
Monaghan, Mr 88
Mooney, Daniel 49
Mooney, James 48
Morrison, County Inspector 26
Mountjoy 22, 23
Movea, Co. Tyrone 75, 77, 85, 86
Moveagh, Co. Tyrone *see* Movea, Co. Tyrone
Musgrave Channel, Belfast 23

National Volunteers 27, 35
Nenagh, Co. Tipperary 28–30, 35
Newbridge College, Co. Kildare 42
Newmills, Co. Tyrone 95
Newsletter 13, 23, 49–51, 62–63, 64, 71, 83, 103

North Channel 6
Northern Ireland xvi
Norway 23

O'Boyle, Constable 93
O'Brien brothers 28–30
O'Connor, Father 88
O'Neill, Head Constable Henry 93, 94
O'Sullivan, Sergeant xxv
O'Toole, Edward 12, 102
Old Glenarm Road, Larne 10, 11
Oldtown Street, Cookstown 37, 50
Omagh, Co. Tyrone 58, 71
Orange Order xiii, 5, 22, 25, 27–28, 32, 34, 37–38, 46, 49, 50–51, 52, 53, 98, 99
Orritor Street, Cookstown 28, 37, 46–49, 51–52
Owens, Dr 61, 62

Parnell, Charles Stewart 97
Passionist Order 10
Pearse, Pádraig xiv
Penal Laws 7
Phoenix Park, Dublin 4, 12
Phoenix, Éamon 62, 102
Pomeroy, Co. Tyrone 61, 62, 83, 100
Portrush, Co. Antrim xxiv
Princess Margaret, SS xxx, 1–2, 12, 13
Princess Victoria, SS 1, 6

Quinn's Lane, Dungannon 95

Redmond, John xiv, 26, 32, 34, 53, 91, 96, 97, 99
Regan, John xviii
Reilly, Minnie 40, 41, 54
Ricardo, General A. xvii
Riordan, James 70–71
Rock, Co. Tyrone 43, 45, 55, 59, 62, 64, 69, 74
  Tullyodonnell Chapel 72
Roscommon, County 22
Royal Irish Constabulary xii–xiii, xiv, xv–xvi, xviii, xix, xx, xxvi, 14, 15, 19, 22, 24, 25, 31, 35, 36, 39, 44, 52, 53, 54, 55, 56, 61, 65, 71, 73, 84, 85, 86, 93, 94, 95–96, 100, 101, 102
  McKenna's career in xii, xiii–xiv, xx–xxii, xxv–xxvi, xxx, 1, 16, 17, 22, 27, 28, 31, 33, 37, 38, 57, 72, 91, 95–96, 97–100
Royal Ulster Constabulary xii, xix, xxvi, 6, 8, 9–10, 12, 13, 14, 53, 101

Salisbury, Lord 97
Scotland xxiv
Second World War 101
Shankill Road, Belfast xiii
Shea, Patrick xv, xviii, xix
Sinn Féin xv, 32, 38, 42, 51, 52, 53, 61–62, 71, 75, 85, 87, 91, 92–93, 94, 95, 97, 99
Small, Mrs 48
Smith, Inspector 26
Smith, James 48
Soloheadbeg, Co. Tipperary xv, 35, 99
St Joseph's Primary, Larne 6
St MacNissi, Church of, Larne xxx, 1, 2, 3, 6, 7, 8, 10, 13
Stephenson, Major Robert xvii
Stewartstown, Co. Tyrone 75
Stormont, Belfast xv
Stranmillis University College, Belfast xviii
Swindall, Constable 37–38, 81–82, 95

Tallents, S.G. xv, xvii, 71
Thurles, Co. Tipperary 30, 35
Tipperary, County 32
Tomb, Cuthbert H. 66
Tralee, Co. Kerry 36
Tripartite Agreement, 1925 101
Troubles, 1919–21 *see* Anglo-Irish War, 1919–21
Tuam, Co. Galway xx
Tullyhogue, Co. Tyrone 56, 58, 73, 76
Tullylagan, Co. Tyrone 83, 84
Turton, William 48, 49
Tuskar Light, Co. Wexford 23
Twadell, W.J. 101
Twelfth of July xxi, 7, 27, 37, 46–53

Tyrone Constitution 51–52, 103
Tyrone Courier 49, 51, 54, 64, 65–67, 69, 83–87, 88, 103
Tyrone, County xii, xvii, xxvi, 34, 53, 54, 60, 61, 62, 63, 67, 69, 70, 71, 77, 86, 88, 91, 103

Ulster Clubs 98
Ulster Crisis, 1914 xiv
Ulster Herald 52, 53, 72, 103
Ulster Solemn League and Covenant 98
Ulster Special Constabulary *see* 'A' Specials, 'B' Specials
Ulster Unionist Council 22
Ulster Unionist Party 98, 100
Ulster Volunteer Force xiii, xiv, xv, xvii, xviii, 16, 19–21, 22, 23–25, 27, 32, 35, 48, 84, 89, 98, 99

Unionist Clubs 19, 20, 34
United Kingdom 99

Victoria, Queen 35

War of Independence, 1919–21 *see* Anglo-Irish War, 1919–21
Webb, Alfred xx
Wilhelm II, Kaiser 26, 35
Wilson, Mr 37, 38, 95
Windsor, J. 48
Windsor, W.J. 48
World War I *see* First World War
World War II *see* Second World War

Young, Sergeant 65

www.ingramcontent.com/pod-product-compliance
Lightning Source LLC
Chambersburg PA
CBHW071627080526
44588CB00010B/1296